MW00451840

TRUTH DECAY

HOW GOVERNMENT CORRUPTION CAUSED A POLITICAL SCANDAL VICTIMIZING TEXAS DENTISTS AND HOW IT COULD HAPPEN TO YOU!

DR. JUAN D. VILLARREAL

TRUTH DECAY
How Government Corruption Caused a Political Scandal
Victimizing Texas Dentists and How It Could Happen to You!

Dr. Juan D. Villarreal

Published by: Texas Dentists for Medicaid Reform

ISBN: 978-0692827055

Copyright © 2017 by Dr. Juan D. Villarreal and Texas Dentists for Medicaid Reform. All rights reserved. No part of this publication may be reproduced, distributed, or transmitted in any form or by any means, including photocopying, recording, or other electronic or mechanical methods, without the prior written permission of the publisher, except in the case of brief quotations embodied in critical reviews and certain other noncommercial uses permitted by copyright law. Contact the publisher for further information at info@tdmr.org.

FOREWORD

This is the true story of the best and worst of human nature. It's about the absolute misappropriation of power by a series of bureaucrats running powerful state agencies without concern for the truth nor the path of destruction left in the wake of their self-gratifying rampage.

If this were a novel, you'd likely be tempted to cast it aside as improbable, if not impossible. Unfortunately for the victims, the story you are about to read is true. There are two sets of victims. On the one hand you have the dentists who were maligned, and in some cases bankrupted, by the vengeful actions of the power-wielding "officials."

The other set of victims numbers over three million strong. Strong only in numbers. Weak in that they are just children. Children born into poor families. Children whom we are bound to protect. Children whose best health interests became an inconvenient cost to state officials whose twisted sense of mission led them far astray from their sworn oaths of duty. Far from "protect and serve." They sought to destroy the very providers of the care desperately needed by the children of the State of Texas.

How is it possible that nobody knew what was going on? Dentists must maintain their license to practice in order to make a living and support themselves and their families. Unfortunately, it's easy for rogue government officials to make life hard for a dentist. The threat of loss of license and practice due to conviction on fraud charges (regardless of whether or not those charges have any basis in truth) weighs like a boulder on the chest and in the minds of the accused.

Furthermore, the *cost* of being accused, the freezing of money already earned but not yet dispersed, can be equally if not more intimidating than the potential court cases and defense of their licenses and good names. Dentists have been afraid or unable to fight back. Nobody was willing to challenge authority. Nobody was willing to stand up for the three million-plus children and *be* their voice. Until now.

This is the story of David and Goliath. This is a tale of *right* and *wrong*. Dr. Juan D. Villarreal was willing to stand up and fight back at great risk and cost to himself. Juan chose to fight back for all of those who could or would not. Juan gave voice to the three million plus children.

Dr. Tom Orent
CEO Gems Publishing, USA, Inc.

FOREWORD

Dr. Tom Orent has lectured at dental schools and societies in 48 of the 50 states and in five countries. He has served as editor of the American Academy of Cosmetic Dentistry Journal and authored four books and hundreds of articles on esthetics and dental practice management. His books, CD's, DVD's, and newsletters have been sold in 47 countries.

TABLE OF CONTENTS

INTRODUCTION

Our constitutional rights are the very foundation of our freedom and our greatness as a nation. Rights such as being considered innocent until proven guilty, not being tried for the same thing more than once, right to trial by a jury of one's peers, and due process are just a few of the basic rights our country's founding fathers envisioned for us. We often take these rights for granted. However, they do define us as a society and are supposed to guarantee that our "God-given" freedoms are protected. This is not just for an elite few but for each and every citizen of the United States.

And when these rights are trampled upon by rogue bureaucrats, individuals, as well as society as a whole, pay an enormous price. This book is what I have experienced and why I have written this story. I want people everywhere to know that rogue bureaucrats, political agendas, and kangaroo courts are very real and still exist in spite of our Constitution. We must be ever vigilant in recognizing and exposing them. Just as terrorism is an external threat to our country, this is an internal threat to our way of life and the freedoms we hold so dear.

I have been a dentist for over thirty-three years with a prospering practice in Texas. A significant portion of my practice has been devoted to taking care of people through Medicaid, which is both a state and federal program that provides healthcare coverage for those with low incomes. Believing that every child should be given an equal chance in life and have access to healthcare, I decided to take Medicaid for children at a time when it was not very popular to do so. In fact, I became one of the few dentists in South Texas who did, providing orthodontic treatment (teeth straightening) as well as general care.

Back in 2011 the Texas state government was paying an extraordinary amount of money for Medicaid and orthodontic claims. One in seven Texans were relying on Medicaid for long-term service and support at that time. Keep in mind that Texas is fundamentally against any entitlement program. And when Obamacare was being introduced, Texas rejected it as it would have cost the state billions of dollars to implement. I believe the Texas government wanted scapegoats for their large Medicaid expenditures to help them recover fees paid out and at the same time send a powerful message to other healthcare providers, discouraging their claims. Adding to their motivation is a very strong financial incentive for the government to go after what may or may not be entitlement program fraud; for every dollar the government spends on enforcement they make back seven! Where else can you get that kind of return?

In 2011 the state was on a witch hunt and in September of that year we received a letter from the Texas inspector general that they were placing a payment hold on all our

Medicaid orthodontic work based on a "credible allegation of fraud" (a provision of Obamacare). They were giving us ten days to respond to the accusation. As you will see later in this book, this allegation is ludicrous since we run a very conscientious practice. Receiving this letter was appalling because we had a lot of children in the middle of treatment that we couldn't ethically or professionally stop seeing, yet the dentists working on the cases needed to get paid. Medicaid payments for orthodontic work represented 25 percent of our office's income; this put an extraordinary amount of financial burden on us. It would be seven months from the start of the payment hold that a hearing was finally scheduled. What ever happened to due process? Interestingly, this was the first hearing ever for a dentist in Texas for a Medicaid fraud payment hold.

This is just the beginning. What followed were more delays, endless depositions, trials, shakedowns, and government agencies writing their own rules and regulations for themselves. They demanded large sums of money to make the harassment go away and other egregious violations of constitutional rights. As of the writing of this book, my case has still not been fully resolved.

While this book is very much about what happened to me, it is also an alarm bell to everyday folks that government agencies can and do get out of control sometimes and violate our constitutional rights in pursuit of their own bureaucratic and political agendas. Just as importantly, this book is also a warning to other healthcare professionals about what can potentially happen to them. Should you be unlucky enough to find yourself in a situation similar to mine, I have provided you with some sage advice and counsel based on my experiences that will benefit you greatly.

May the truth set you free ...

CHAPTER 1

WHAT IS HAPPENING TO THE AMERICAN DREAM?

This is a true story of villains, heroes, children, bureaucrats, and justice. It involves big money, big government, and innocent lives. The circumstances I relate have impacted many hard-working, upstanding people, crossed racial lines as well as political ones, and left a devastation of financial loss for many. While it happened to me in Texas, it is occurring in other states too.

It is really about the American dream, which I know can be achieved. Coming from a very modest background, I worked hard and climbed the ladder of professional and financial success. This has made me very proud to set the example for others in my community.

This story is ultimately about the threats to that dream. It is not about the threats we read about daily—terrorism, immigration, globalization, radical religions.

It is singularly about threats coming from those we have entrusted to govern us, those who are supposed to keep our Constitution alive and those who guarantee our rights in this country.

Yes, we have our cherished constitutional rights—due process, innocent until proven guilty, trial by a jury of our peers—apparently. Most of us will take these for granted if we live a normal, productive life and never have cause to think about them or depend on them.

Yet, every day we hear news stories of other people accused of crimes and think "probably guilty." We have been conditioned into believing that events are as depicted in the media.

That is the way I had become. But I became disabused of this notion very quickly a few years ago when suddenly my constitutional rights were violated and it had dramatic impact on my dental practice, my patients, and my personal life.

Aside from being a warning, this book is information about what to do if something like this happens to you —a successful American, no matter your race, religion, or creed.

Believe me, it is a great shock to find out that those rights you were educated to believe you have aren't there for you.

How are these rights being subverted? Quite simply, there are now government agencies writing regulations for themselves that have the force of law and can defy our constitutional guarantees. They are not passed by any legislature or elected representatives. Everyone has heard or knows about civil and criminal law. But it is administrative law, the law which has been developed to manage government agencies, under which such evils can take place.

Worse, this practice can facilitate rogue bureaucrats who, for their own glory and power, use these self-written regulations to harm citizens and taxpayers and bring financial ruin with little to no consequences for themselves. In fact, they are protected by the state because they are granted immunity for acting as agents of the state.

All of a sudden there is no due process. There is no innocent until proven guilty. There is no right to a speedy trial by a jury of one's peers.

There is only a shakedown. A demand for a large amount of money to stop the harassment so they will go away. Guilt, innocence, or law has nothing to do with it. The implicit threat is "comply or go bankrupt."

There is no recourse *except* to fight back *at your own expense*!

And for that reason, this story is offered to you as a fascinating tale, a weapon, and an example of what to expect and what to do if you ever need it.

CHAPTER 2
ADVERSITY TO SUCCESS

To give this story the proper context, it is important to tell you something of myself and my background.

I am a healthcare professional, a dentist by profession, who has over the last thirty-three years built a successful practice in my hometown of Harlingen, Texas. In fact, through my hard work and dedication and the contributions of many wonderful patients, competent fellow dentists, hygienists, and staff, I built the largest single office practice in Texas, which has now expanded to six other satellite offices.

But I don't count personal success as everything. I believe you have to give back too.

So as a result of my twenty-two years of schooling, which helped me to realize my American dream, I became an advocate for education and served on the local school board. I promoted the teaching of morals and ethics through character-building classes for students using precepts such as "set a good example" and "safeguard and improve your environment."

The students then applied these lessons in our area by doing special projects of their own which were reviewed and judged by community leaders. Scholarships were awarded to the top students who created an impact in our community. A special awards ceremony was held to acknowledge all participants and reward the winners. Many of these students have now themselves grown up to be outstanding professionals and community leaders.

Due to my own experiences as a healthcare professional working in the emergency room at the Houston Medical Center and seeing the plight of others created by debilitating drug abuse, I founded Narconon South Texas, a not-for-profit drug rehabilitation facility which has proven successful in helping many recover from the ravages of drug abuse. The facility has grown to an eighteen-acre plat in a tranquil location right outside of Harlingen and helps addicts from across both the US and Mexico get back their lives.

I have served as president of the Harlingen Economic Development Board and worked with local leaders to bring economic opportunities to our community. As president, I participated in the groundbreaking ceremony for the Regional Academic Health Center that now houses the University of Texas Rio Grande Valley School of Medicine in Harlingen—the first medical school in the Rio Grande Valley.

I have been president of the Hispanic Dental Association. I joined this organization when I was a dental student because of their purpose to help the Hispanic community. Their mission statement is "As the leading voice for Hispanic oral health we provide service, education, advocacy, and leadership for elimination of oral health disparities in the Hispanic community." Since 1999, I have sponsored the Juan D. Villarreal scholarship to support promising HDA dental, dental hygiene, and dental lab students as they pursue their academic training.

In 2001, Governor Rick Perry appointed me to the Texas State Board of Dental Examiners, which regulates the practice of dentistry in the state. I served on the board from 2001- 2008 in several capacities—secretary of the board, chair of the Enforcement Committee, and member of the Legislative Committee. As secretary, I had the privilege to review over 1,400 cases and make recommendations for their handling. It was work for many long nights and weekends.

Well, that is the success that comes from a lot of hard work and overcoming years of adversity.

I have always loved helping our community and particularly its indigent children. I know what these children go through as I had been there myself. My mom and dad had only a second- and third-grade education, respectively, and we had eight in the family.

My parents exhibited a strong work ethic and made it possible for us to become enrolled in a private catholic school. Their example provided a strong foundation for my future success.

Unfortunately, my father died of cancer when I was thirteen years old. Our family had to come together to make ends meet. My brothers and sisters and I found jobs after school and during the summers to help support the household. Even though we were in the lower socioeconomic strata, we never considered ourselves poor. We had good health and the vigor of youth to carry us forward in life.

During my grade school years, there was a division among English- and Spanish-speaking students. I started school not knowing English with English-speaking teachers. I was fortunate enough to succeed when many Hispanic students were labeled Special Ed because of language barriers.

In high school, I was told by a counselor not to consider going to college because "college would be too difficult for me." I refused to believe that. She may not have had a clue as to the amount of time I was working to help my family and how persistent I was on reaching my goals. By good graces, I was able to overcome barriers and not be influenced by negative opinions.

After high school, I went to the Valley Baptist Hospital School of Radiologic Technology and started on my path as a professional by becoming an x-ray technician. This held me in good standing through my time in the US Army at Fort Sam Houston in San Antonio, Texas.

Because I was an x-ray technician and the military had a "stripes for skills" program, I received the rank of Specialist 5 which is the equivalent of a Sergeant E-5.

But this did not go down so well with the staff sergeant who had been there for sixteen years and whom I was only one grade below. He made my primary occupation cleaning latrines, mopping floors, and the like.

I was eventually given the opportunity to work with Colonel Louis B. Levy, who had a PhD in radiation physics. During the time I worked with him, he trained me to be his assistant on radiation physics and radiation dosimetry (measuring dosage of radiation) of cancer patients. Col. Levy was a great mentor and father figure for me. He always validated my potential and encouraged me to continue my education. I developed great respect and admiration for his caring attitude and intelligence.

So I completed my three-year stint in the U.S. Army with two years of college and was fully trained in radiation dosimetry. I was one of only two individuals in the state with special training in this area. Despite an offer from the military to stay and work in civil service, I decided to continue my education.

Three years later in 1979, I embarked on my career in dentistry at the University of Texas Health Science Center at San Antonio with the assistance of the GI Bill. I observed certain attitudes towards minorities that were occurring at the time. For example, the dental school, from my recollection, had only ever had twenty-six African American students in the program. None of them had graduated. The attrition rate among Mexican Americans was 50 percent and for women it was 35 percent at that time.

During dental school, most of the lab work grading was subjective and if you had a biased professor your grades suffered regardless of the work you put in. I found myself working twice as hard but still ending up with a lower grade. It was a common experience to have friendly students come up and look at my work and comment with surprise that my grades were lower.

We even had a game we played in dental school where we would take our work to another instructor and we would get a totally different grade with different things to correct. The good news was that the majority of the professors were excellent and it was a small minority that we had trouble with.

During my time in dental school, I focused on the application of knowledge, not grades. I probably did more clinical procedures than anybody else in my class, even after I had completed all my requirements.

While attending dental school, I also served in the U.S. Army Reserves and spent one weekend a month and six weeks during the summer working as a dentist on military personnel at Fort Sam Houston in San Antonio. This army experience enhanced my dental education as I was able to work directly with professors from the dental school. This gave me plenty of experience. It was also great that I got paid, which helped me support my mom back home.

When I started my practice in 1983 in Harlingen, I encountered economic barriers rather than language barriers. There were only two other Hispanic dentists in the area. When I went around seeking to work in another practice to start off, I was dissuaded from doing so and told to work outside the valley because "there were already too many dentists" in the area.

I eventually had to start my own practice due to these challenges. The local established banks wouldn't loan me money, so I found a startup bank willing to lend me $30,000. I ended up becoming very ingenious at saving money and finding low-cost solutions to establish my office and keep it running. For example, I found that I could use a Sears vacuum pump and compressor to run my dental equipment, which worked about as well but cost one-tenth of those sold by dental supply companies.

Once I started my practice, I wanted to give back to the community that I was born into and felt proud to be able to serve with my newly acquired dental skills, so I made a conscious decision to participate in Medicaid and treat poor children eligible for the program. Medicaid started in 1965 and is a federal program that is jointly paid for by both federal and state governments to provide healthcare for indigent families, among other groups.

Like many Americans, I don't really believe in entitlement programs, but we have public schools for everybody because we want to give every child an equal chance to get ahead. I think it should be the same with healthcare for children. Hence, my decision to take Medicaid at a time when it was not popular. In fact, I was one of the few dentists in South Texas who did and also provided orthodontic treatment—straightening seriously crooked teeth—under the program. The reimbursement rates paid by the state were very low but the need was so great.

Throughout the years, the number of children we would provide dental services to continued to grow. At the beginning of 2012, Medicaid treatment for youth amounted to 50 percent of our practice and about 50 percent of that was for orthodontic treatment.

We always ensured every child qualified, filled out the forms correctly, got prior authorizations for the treatment if we needed to, and did the right work. In order to ensure those receiving state aid for braces qualified under state guidelines, Texas Medicaid established a process for dentists to receive permission before braces were ever placed. We always followed this process exactly before ever placing braces on a patient. We had absolutely no problems for twenty-eight years. When we found something wrong, such as a billing error, we even self-reported and sent the state back a check.

Then, things changed at the end of 2011 for myself and many other dentists in Texas and the children we were treating.

CHAPTER 3

MEDICAID IN TEXAS, VERY UNHEALTHY

Let me explain some of the basics of Medicaid for you. The following is not too technical and you might want to know something about how our healthcare system works. Even though I have been a Medicaid provider since 1983, I wasn't totally familiar with it all either.

Texas Medicaid and CHIP (Children's Health Insurance Program) in Perspective, 10th Edition, published by the Texas Health and Human Services Commission, also known as the "Pink book," tells us:

"Medicaid is a jointly funded state-federal healthcare program, established in Texas in 1967 and administered by the Health and Human Services Commission (HHSC). In order to participate in Medicaid, federal law requires states to cover certain population groups (mandatory eligibility groups) and gives them the flexibility to cover other population groups (optional eligibility groups). Each state chooses its own eligibility criteria within federal minimum standards. States can apply to the Centers for Medicare & Medicaid Services (CMS) for a waiver of federal law to expand health coverage beyond these groups. Medicaid is an entitlement program, which means the federal government does not, and a state cannot, limit the number of eligible people who can enroll, and Medicaid must pay for any services covered under the program. In July 2013, about one in seven Texans (3.7 million of the 26.4 million) relied on Medicaid for health coverage or long-term services and supports."

I learned that not every state approves dental services for the program. In Texas, impoverished children under twenty-one are eligible for dental care. In fact, Texas boasts that "Medicaid also provides a broader array of acute health services to children than do most private health plans, such as dental benefits."

That all sounds good except Texas, despite having to manage the Medicaid program, doesn't have a great record of supporting it.

Back in 1993, a couple of parents sued the state in federal court because it was not living up to providing basic healthcare services, including dental care, mandated by its obligation under Medicaid. Texas was willing to take federal money but was not willing to provide proper care. This is called the *Frew* lawsuit as it was brought by Linda Frew on behalf of her daughter Carla. It became a class-action suit on behalf of all Medicaid-eligible children in Texas.

In 1996, an eighty-page court-ratified settlement was reached, but the state didn't implement it to correct the problems.

So by 1999, the state was back in court and fought enforcement of the settlement agreement all the way to the Supreme Court. It wasn't until 2007, when the Supreme Court denied a motion to review the case, that Texas was forced to pony up on the settlement agreement.

That's not all.

Texas is legendary for its opposition to the expansion of Medicaid under the Affordable Care Act. Even though the state would receive $65 billion more in federal funds over ten years, former Governor Rick Perry wanted no part of it. Instead of expanding Medicaid, because of the "ineptitude" of the federal government, Perry wanted to have the feds give Texas block grants and total control over its own program. This opposition to Medicaid expansion is still a plank in the current government of Governor Greg Abbott.

But you'll notice nobody is really talking about it anymore. The reason is that Texas has had some small "ineptitude" itself, as you'll soon find out.

It is this loosening of the purse strings in 2007 that really started all the problems for myself and other dentists, especially with Medicaid orthodontic treatment. Dental reimbursement rates for some services were raised—some by 100 percent. More dentists joined the ranks of those taking Medicaid patients. Dental chains, or dental practices with multiple offices, some operating nationally, such as Kool Smiles and Jefferson Dental, were there. Texas-only chains such as All Smiles and Navarro Orthodontics started and grew.

For orthodontic treatment, the rates didn't change. However, as more dentists joined the program, more children were seen who had been approved for orthodontic treatment.

Here are some simple facts that you need to know about the Medicaid orthodontic program because it is important to this story.

1. Before any orthodontic treatment could begin, every child treated under the program had to have their full treatment plan pre-approved by the state's Medicaid private sector contractor, the Texas Medicaid and Healthcare Partnership (or TMHP), to make sure the child was eligible for treatment. This is a Medicaid requirement. TMHP was run by Xerox, which was awarded the contract in 2004. The approval process required the dentist to provide a treatment plan with:
   a. a scoring sheet,
   b. teeth models (not required between Aug 2004-Oct 2011),
   c. radiographs (full set of x-rays), and
   d. photographs of the child's face, jaw, and tooth structure.

2. If TMHP didn't approve a request, the doctor was usually not reimbursed for the costs of the application, which could be up to several hundred dollars as complete patient records had to be submitted

(x-rays, etc.). Only two out of every ten cases that were not approved were paid.

3. Even if a dentist did not think a child's condition was severe enough to be covered by the Medicaid program, the dentist was required by TMHP to send in the application anyway for review. This was because it was TMHP's job to determine which children qualified and which children didn't. The dentist did not have the authority to decide this.

4. A full course of orthodontic treatment, given over two years, to a Medicaid child would cost the state, on average, $2,500 in 2011. This is about half the cost of treatment for private-pay patients, which would, on average, be $5,000.

By the fall of 2011, because of the demand for orthodontic services, I had three dentists in my practice who were treating Medicaid children. Two of them, Dr. George Franklin and Dr. Cuong Van Nguyen, were specialists or orthodontists. Dr. Nguyen was also board certified. The other was my business partner, Dr. Vivian Teegardin, who is a general dentist that does orthodontic work because she loves it.

THINGS TO REMEMBER:

1. Texas is fundamentally opposed to entitlement programs such as Medicaid yet has to pay their share of the costs and manage the federal program.

2.   Texas has the option to opt out of participating in Medicaid. Every state does. They choose not to because the state wants the matching funds.

3.   The Texas Health and Human Services Commission is the mega-agency that oversees healthcare and Medicaid in Texas.

4.   Texas reluctantly started pouring more money into Medicaid for child healthcare services, including dental services, in 2007 because of the Supreme Court. It didn't really want to do this.

5.   The Texas Health and Human Services Commission oversaw this expenditure through its contractor, the Texas Medicaid and Healthcare Partnership. Xerox was the parent company of TMHP.

Now that you have some background about Medicaid in Texas, let's get on to the rest of the story.

CHAPTER 4

MEDIA + POLITICS = THE PERFECT STORM

In the late spring of 2011, I started to hear rumblings in the dental community about orthodontic clinics in Dallas being accused of Medicaid fraud.

Although our practice is in the Rio Grande Valley, one of the local doctors, Dr. Carlos Navarro, had offices located in Dallas. So it came to our attention because a number of Dallas dentists started sending out e-mails to their colleagues about news reports coming out on WFAA, the Dallas TV station, which was well-known for its investigative reporting. The news stories were available on YouTube so we saw them. Some clinics were being accused of advertising free braces for Medicaid-eligible children on big signs in front of their offices.

WFAA TV's noted investigative reporter Byron Harris had done some legwork and found that Texas was spending more on Medicaid orthodontic treatment than the other top ten states combined. The "free braces" advertisements were a symptom of a program out of control. This level of spending in Texas was way more than that of the state's political and economic rivals, California and New York.

WFAA reported that Texas in 2010 spent $184 million on Medicaid orthodontic treatment while California only spent $19 million and New York $61 million.

Harris later claimed that Texas was spending more than the other forty-nine states combined, but this claim was eventually deemed a half-truth by the political watchdog website Politifact. It turns out Harris made the claim without having the spending figures from all fifty states.

Regardless, his "more than the rest of the country combined" became a war cry for Texas politicians outraged by the spending on the program.

Imagine an entitlement-program-unfriendly state like Texas spending so much money on poor children's crooked teeth. It could only be fraud! Somebody had to have put a fast one over on them. Somebody needed to pay!

So the story rolled out.

WFAA ended up doing a series of stories—over thirty-five from May 2011 to April 2013—and Harris was given a number of press awards for his coverage. But when dentists such as myself wanted to get the other side of the story told, he wasn't very interested. But other media outlets were, thankfully.

Back in those early days, I never expected this would have anything to do with us.

Not only was Dallas far away, we had just sent a check of $129,808.11 back to Medicaid because we found that TMHP, the claims administrator, had mistakenly paid us for claims for children who were also covered by private insurance. You would never think that Medicaid kids would have private dental insurance but in some divorce cases, the non-primary custodial parent is required to provide dental insurance by court order. Medicaid was only supposed to pay for the amount the private insurance did not cover, but instead paid the whole bill.

This overpayment was discovered by one of our managers while auditing patient accounts. Upon discovery, we had an all-hands action by our staff to trace back every Medicaid account to find the exact amount owed back to TMHP. The complete project took about a month of work by three staff with a final review by their senior to finally determine the full amount. We then wrote the check and sent it back to the state. We never received any acknowledgement from TMHP about the repayment, although we knew they received it because the check was cashed by our local bank.

So in mid-July 2011, I was surprised to find an investigator from the Health and Human Services Commission Office of Inspector General (OIG) in the reception area of our office. He had an investigative demand to get the case files of 160 of our Medicaid orthodontic patients. We had three days to copy them off and get them ready.

Well, it was the law so we complied. I didn't expect much to come of it; we keep excellent records.

A shock came at the beginning of September though. We received a letter from OIG telling us that they were placing a "credible allegation of fraud" payment hold on 100 percent of our Medicaid orthodontic billings. We had ten days to respond.

This was outrageous. I was floored. This action cut 25 percent of our income right there, immediately. Plus, we still had a lot of children under treatment and couldn't professionally end or stop their treatment. That would be unconscionable. Yet the dentists doing the work had to be paid. So we became cash-strapped.

We had to reorganize our office to be able to handle the loss we were experiencing due to the payment hold in order to make ends meet. It took a lot of work and ingenuity to pay overhead expenses. We really had to change our operating basis over the next several years to continue to stay viable.

When the payment hold was placed, it was very stressful for me personally because the OIG wasn't going after the dental staff who provided the actual work in my clinic. They were instead coming after me, the practice owner, which I couldn't understand because I hadn't seen the patients in question.

I later learned that this was a tactic used by the OIG and promoted by the chief villain of this piece, Jack Stick, the head of enforcement for this agency. In March of 2012, he participated in a webinar on Medicaid fraud put on by the National Conference of State Legislatures and said that he had reorganized his enforcement efforts to "go where the money is."

After receiving the notice, I immediately engaged several excellent lawyers—Oscar Garcia and Tony Canales—

and we resolved to get an expedited hearing on the matter. Tony Canales is a litigation lawyer, recommended as one of the best. Oscar is a friend of mine and we both served as members of the Texas State Board of Dental Examiners from 2001 to 2008. He knows dental issues. Later, in May 2013, Oscar was appointed to serve as a district judge in Cameron County by Governor Perry and was not able to represent our office.

When that occurred, we hired an outstanding, young administrative law attorney from Austin, Jason Ray. Jason has continued to be my attorney to this day and has become, in my mind, the leading legal expert in Texas on Medicaid payment holds.

It is Jason who finally, after several years, forced the state to return the funds about which I am writing here. Returning them was something Jack Stick said they would never do. Jason is now the go-to guy for many Medicaid providers.

But an expedited hearing? No such luck.

After depositions and delays, it didn't happen until April 2012—seven months after the start of the payment hold. And my hearing was the first ever payment hold hearing for any dentist in the state accused of "fraud."

CHAPTER 5
TRIALS AND TRIBULATIONS

The lead-up to the trial was pretty uneventful despite the seriousness of the charges. Except for the major financial burden we had been placed under due to the payment hold, it seemed like we would come through this OK.

While OIG had taken away 160 patient files when they first entered our office, for the hearing they were now using just 85 cases.

For our defense, we had hired an expert witness to review these cases. Dr. Jim Orr had been the dental director under the previous Medicaid contractor before TMHP/Xerox took over in 2004. Dr. Orr had also worked with the Health and Human Services Commission for over ten years on the investigation of dental fraud. When he was dental director, he reviewed all our orthodontic submissions during his tenure and gave us direction on which cases qualified and which cases didn't.

For our case, he was very helpful as he found that he would have approved all of our cases except eight. In a number of the cases, he actually rated the orthodontic conditions more serious than our own dentists. This was very positive for us. He didn't find any fraud whatsoever.

There was the customary round of depositions before the April hearing.

The attorneys who were prosecuting the case for OIG, Corrie Alvarado and John Medlock, were quite pleasant to deal with. They deposed our orthodontic providers, Dr. Orr, and me. I found that they accorded us a great deal of professional respect.

We ended up deposing their expert witness, Dr. Charles Evans, and Billy Millwee, who was then the head of Medicaid for Texas.

During the deposition, off the record, I asked Mr. Millwee if he knew how many children and dentists were being hurt by the payment holds. He replied that he didn't know of any. I was surprised. Here's the head of Texas Medicaid without any knowledge or consciousness of what was going on to the people involved in this debacle. This left me with a bad impression of bureaucrats who, like Millwee, retire after creating problems for the state and then go on to be hired by the private sector as consultants. Millwee retired in August 2012.

The strange thing was that the state's expert witness, Dr. Evans, was an exceptionally well-respected Austin orthodontist but he wasn't even board certified. Our own Dr. Nguyen was.

We also discovered through deposing him that in his long career of over forty years as an orthodontist, Dr. Evans had never, ever taken on a single Medicaid patient. He knew absolutely nothing about it. He had absolutely no experience with the Texas Medicaid Manual or filling out the prior authorization request forms that were submitted to Xerox. Our own dentists had almost twenty years of combined experience in this area.

Yet he had concluded, after reviewing our patients' case files, that eighty-four out of eight-five patients in the OIG sample did not qualify under Texas Medicaid rules.

The primary bone of contention between Dr. Evans, the state, and our dentists had to do with something called the Handicapping Labial-Lingual Deviation (HLD) score sheet, which is filled out by a dentist based on his observation of the patient's condition and indicates the severity of how crooked the teeth are. This sheet is one of the forms that is filled out as part of the submission for prior authorization from TMHP/Xerox to treat the patient.

The HLD score sheet is a numerical index of orthodontic problems that are counted up and totaled. A score of twenty-six or more means the patient has enough of an orthodontic problem for dental work to be considered a medical necessity and to have treatment funded by Medicaid. This was an arbitrary number and during depositions we discovered that the dental director for TMHP approved a high percentage of cases even if the patient did not score twenty-six points.

On the scoring of these sheets, there was only one item for dispute between the state's expert, our expert, and our dentists. It was something called an "ectopic eruption," the definition of which was a highly subjective component and open to professional interpretation. For the sake of simplicity, it refers to a tooth that is abnormally positioned in the jaw bone, usually rotated or slanted.

In March of 2012, right before my hearing, HHSC issued a bulletin to Medicaid dentists claiming it was now clarifying the definition of ectopic eruption. In fact, the agency was now retroactively changing it so that very few patients would qualify for treatment, making it almost impossible for a provider to prove their innocence in court against allegations of Medicaid fraud. This change itself was fraudulent.

We thought that Evan's conclusion on our cases was ridiculous and couldn't understand why OIG was relying on it.

We came to understand that Dr. Evan's hiring and willingness to participate as an expert witness had more to do with his political view of Medicaid as an unwanted entitlement program than any real expertise he had to determine dental Medicaid fraud. This became evident from his deposition because he was never asked to determine if any of our dentists had committed fraud. Yet he was supposed to determine if we had violated Medicaid standards, which he had no experience with but was certainly willing to expound upon for his expert witness fee. He was simply there to push the state's case against dentists who they wanted to scapegoat for their large expenditure on Medicaid for orthodontic treatment.

Although we had a very uneventful trial, there was one notable incident. At the end of the first day of the hearing, two OIG employees showed up at the back of the courtroom. My lawyer, upon seeing them, exclaimed to the other lawyers present something like "Who in the hell are they?"

That day in the courtroom there were numerous state attorneys sitting in the front row and after some sniggering and not-so-flattering comments by the OIG lawyers, it turned out the dynamic duo were none other than Jack Stick, then OIG's deputy inspector general for enforcement, our chief villain introduced earlier, and his right-hand man, Cody Cazares.

Stick, although he only joined OIG in June of 2011, had already gained a substantial and somewhat fierce reputation. He was a former Texas house representative for House District 50, an area including north Austin, and had been a City of Bee Caves municipal court judge who left under cloudy circumstances. In 2010 he was found to be improperly dismissing traffic cases in exchange for contributions to the City of Bee Caves. He did not stand for a second appointment as a judge.

It was rumored he was hired for OIG at the request of Governor Rick Perry just after the WFAA investigative reports went public in 2011 as it is said he told the staff at OIG that he worked for Perry, not the then Inspector General Doug Wilson.

Early in his tenure at OIG, Stick carried a stuffed wolf around with him when he had meetings with Medicaid providers, a profound statement on his style and mindset.

Anyway, other than that one incident, which didn't have any bearing on the hearing, things went pretty well.

Indeed, they went excellently!

It took a while. But finally, in August 2012, almost a year from the date our payment hold was placed, Judge Shannon Kilgore, the administrative judge from the State Office of Administrative Hearings, came out with a damning judgment against the state's case and fully exonerated us from allegations of fraud.

She found that:

- Dr. Evan had treated no Medicaid patients and had no familiarity with the HLD score sheet prior to his work on this case.
- For decades in Texas Medicaid practice, prior authorization was granted and benefits paid based on an interpretation of the definition of ectopic eruption that was more expansive than the one employed by Dr. Evans in his review of the HFD cases. The judge was astute enough to realize the changed definition would not fly since it was much more restrictive and not the definition that was in the Medicaid manual.
- Dr. Evans' view of ectopic eruption and his scoring of the patients at issue lack *credibility, reliability, and indicia of reliability* and do not verify the allegations of fraud against HFD.
- There was no evidence that is credible, reliable, or verifying, or that has indicia of reliability that a fraudulent lack of dysfunction existed among the 85 HFD patients reviewed by Dr. Evans.
- There is no evidence that is credible, reliable, or verifying, or that has indicia of reliability that HFD committed fraud or misrepresentation.

We were gratified. Although the judge also found that the eight cases Dr. Orr disagreed with might not qualify for Medicaid, she found absolutely no fraud.

We thought it was over and that the payment hold would be lifted; we would get our money back from the hold and the case would disappear.

We were dead wrong. It was only the beginning.

CHAPTER 6
AGENCY RULES

Yes, we thought it was all over.

Then I found out there was more to the process. This judge's decision was not yet final because the OIG could now send Judge Kilgore reasons why she should change her mind. She had to review those and then finalize her judgment.

But that wasn't all. It then had to be approved or changed by the Health and Human Services Commission itself—an uncanny arrangement. The guys prosecuting you get to approve or disapprove the findings of the impartial court. Other Texas agencies don't have this luxury. HHSC even had its own court for the purpose!

The guys at OIG were angry.

They wanted the judge to retry the case, but she wouldn't have anything to do with that. However, it wasn't until October that she was finally finished and sent her judgment over to HHSC for its approval.

The guys at OIG were angry at me, too.

Two days after Judge Kilgore sent that decision over to HHSC in October, I had two senior OIG investigators in my office demanding more files. They weren't looking for anything having to do with orthodontic treatment. This time they wanted Medicaid patient files having to do with general and pediatric dental treatment.

At the same time as this was occurring, Jack Stick and Doug Wilson were over in Austin telling legislators that if providers were committing fraud in orthodontics, they would also be committing fraud in general dentistry.

So it appeared that since they couldn't find any orthodontic fraud in my practice, they were now retaliating against us by broadening their investigation.

It was obviously a fishing expedition but our office staff dutifully collected the files and spent countless hours doing so, sometimes until 2:00 a.m.

They also asked to interview twenty of our staff who were not allowed to have an attorney present nor record or take notes during the interview.

The sheer volume of records we gave them towered about ten feet in height. It included all the training materials for our staff and information on management tools we use to run the practice. We copied and produced it all within their three-day limit. Jack Stick from Austin was apparently adding more items every day till the last minute, making it more demanding on my staff.

Now I was going to have to wait to find out what more I was going to have to face.

Back at the HHSC Appeals Court, where our decision had gone to, their administrative judge, Susan Fekety, eventually upheld our favorable decision. But we heard rumors of a lot of pressure being thrown at the judge and that Jack

Stick was over in HHSC constantly trying to influence what was going on. There must have been a lot of pressure because Fekety announced her retirement two days after finalizing our decision.

It was now January 2013! Almost a year and a half since this strangulating payment hold was placed and we were struggling. OIG now had accumulated approximately $1.5 million, which we needed to continue to operate.

Thankfully, this decision was finalized and I anticipated getting our money back—the state could only withhold it based on "credible allegations of fraud." These no longer existed.

Wrong again.

HHSC and OIG had made a rule for itself that they could withhold monies for alleged Medicaid program violations. There were no federal or state statutes that backed this up. It was a "rule" that they just made up on their own. It appeared to me that they just wanted to suppress any challenge to their system and they would not tolerate someone being found innocent of their allegations.

Apparently, the only way you could get them to void a "rule" was to take them to a court of law.

What? A government agency can set its own laws that are not passed by Congress or a state legislature and I have to take them to a court of law to prove that it is *not* a law?

Unbelievable!

It took me a while to get this through my head and to take them to court. I didn't want to spend the money either. But I did.

In May of 2014, I filed two lawsuits. The first one was to get the money back that they shouldn't have kept. The second was to get a court to rule on their fake "rule" that they were using to allow them to keep it.

I won't bore you with the details but the bottom line is that we ended up winning on both counts in District Court in Austin and also upon appeal.

I finally got a check from the state just before Christmas in 2014.

This was gratifying. I had taken the bull by the horns and invalidated both of these agency "rules" that were harming not only myself but had the potential to harm all Medicaid providers in Texas.

I realized that the ability of such agencies and their entitled bureaucrats to impose such false laws upon us was a grave threat to our democratic and constitutional way of life. While we won on the legal side of the ledger this time, I concluded this agency was in clear need of reform.

Oh, I should mention that I received my check just after Jack Stick resigned in disgrace from the Health and Human Services Commission.

This was a major victory for Medicaid providers.

CHAPTER 7
ROGUE BUREAUCRATS FALL

Let me tell you all about Jack Stick. He was the epitome of an arrogant, self-centered, full-of-himself bureaucrat. In his eyes, he could do no wrong. But it turned out, he could only do wrong and it was his undoing.

I met with Stick officially for the first time in April of 2013, two months after we had won our decision and had it approved by the HHSC judge. It was at an informal settlement conference that I had asked for to see if I could end this unnecessary continuance of our case.

During early 2013 there was a legislative session in Texas. Texas has them every two years and during them, there is a torrent of new legislation, committee meetings, and hearings going on almost every day for months.

Stick and his boss, the Inspector General Doug Wilson, had been going around telling any committee that would listen to them that Medicaid dental fraud was costing the state anywhere from $650 million to $1 billion per year per their "experts" who were also saying that the Medicaid dental records they looked at showed a 99 percent error rate by Texas dentists. And thus, Stick was promoting that he needed more money from the legislature for more investigators and new Medicaid fraud detection software.

Because politicians had been so embarrassed by the media exposés on the alleged dental Medicaid fraud with orthodontic treatment, they listened raptly and ended up giving them what they wanted.

So Stick's star status had risen in April of 2013 when I met with him.

Although there were lots of other OIG lawyers in the room at the HHSC offices in Austin in which we met, he was the only one who spoke. It was his court and he was king.

I first asked about the second investigation they started when the investigators showed up two days after our judgment was affirmed in October 2012. He said at that time, "no news is good news."

Then we spoke about the orthodontic cases.

As his case against my dental practice had been decimated by the judgment we had obtained, Stick said he wouldn't demand back the full $7.7 million they had been demanding. He was willing to compromise. He would settle for 35 percent of that amount, oh, some $2.6 million.

When I brought up the fact that we had won in court, he swept his hand and said that he now had new experts who would testify for the state, meaning they would come up with something.

"If Jesus Christ were a Medicaid provider, I could find a program violation on him," he proudly exclaimed.

He also told me, "You will never get your payment hold money back because if we give it back to you, it will make us look bad."

He apparently never realized how offensive and idiotic such statements were. I felt like I was talking to the devil himself. I heard later on that he made this "Jesus Christ" comment proudly, to many people—obviously thinking it was a great quote just like that stuffed wolf he used to carry around.

Shortly afterward, the meeting ended with Stick solemnly asking me to think about his offer and questioning me to ensure the meeting went well. He didn't want to be thought of as rude.

I told him, "No, not rude, but inflexible."

Stick's star status continued to rise through 2013 and he was eventually promoted to the position of chief counsel of the entire Health and Human Services Commission—their top legal officer.

Did I mention that his wife, Erica, also worked at the Health and Human Services Commission? She was the chief of staff to the executive commissioner, Kyle Janek. But nepotism was the least of Stick's and HHSC's problems. And he had laid the groundwork for his public downfall a few weeks before our meeting.

In early September 2012, he was arrested and charged with DWI in downtown Austin after leaving a restaurant. The police dash cam video showed Stick's vehicle speeding and veering on the road, which caused the officer to stop him.

Although Stick said he wasn't inebriated, he refused to take the sobriety tests and forced the officer to arrest him, impound his vehicle, and hold him overnight until he was released on a $2,000 bail. Stick refused a blood test but he was forced to provide a sample. Ultimately it led to his conviction, but that didn't occur until four years later. His lawyers were creative on delaying his trial, trying to get him off on a technicality. Something he would never let a Medicaid provider do. He was a hypocrite.

The funniest thing was to hear Stick in that video, the deputy inspector general for enforcement, the top law enforcement official at OIG, tell the Austin police officer that he didn't believe in sobriety tests and that police commonly used them to improperly arrest people. His lack of respect for law enforcement was extremely amusing considering his position.

Stick had kept his arrest quiet but it finally hit the Austin media in November when both the *Texas Tribune* and *Austin American-Statesman* published the story. Stick, true to form, told reporters that he would be vindicated and blood tests would show him innocent. He could lie pretty easily.

The thing that ultimately led to his final downfall and resignation in December of 2014 was a series of deceptions.

Remember that Medicaid anti-fraud software that he wanted to buy for his department? Well, it was from an Austin company, 21CT, which didn't have any experience in fraud detection in Medicaid. But he had become friends with its CEO, a vivacious and attractive woman by the name of Irene Williams.

Stick apparently bypassed the state's normal contract bidding process to get 21CT a $20 million contract through a state contracting program that usually made purchases of only several thousand dollars. 21CT's contract was set to expand to $110 million at the end of 2014 when the no-bid nature of the contract came to media attention.

The final stick that broke Stick's back and led to his resignation was that one of his longtime friends and a former business partner of his was a lobbyist for the company.

So, again, the Texas government was embarrassed and Stick's resignation started a tsunami of investigations from Governor Greg Abbott, HHSC itself, and the State Auditor's Office. It even had interest from the FBI.

Ultimately, there was a tsunami of resignations too. After Stick went Doug Wilson, who was already in hot water, Stick's wife Erica, Stick's former assistant Cody Cazares, a few others, and ultimately it rolled up to Executive Commissioner of HHSC Kyle Janek.

Oh, yes, it affected Doug Wilson's wife too. She worked at HHSC and was put on administrative leave the same month her husband was forced to resign. However, after being on this leave for fifteen months and paid nearly $150,000, she was reinstated to her position as a procurement officer at the Texas Department of Family and Protective Services. She had a nice vacation at taxpayers' expense.

Janek was rightly ousted as a poor manager and took the fall. I would have thought that as a medical doctor he would have had a better appreciation of due process for providers.

Unfortunately, he followed the political agenda that was pulling the strings in this situation.

But is mismanagement in Texas hard to believe?
Not really.

CHAPTER 8

GOOD PEOPLE GET HURT

This was all very disturbing with Stick. I am just glad that our practice was not 100 percent based on Medicaid or just Medicaid orthodontics as a lot of other large practices in Texas had been.

It was Stick who determined to go after the large billers and automatically label them fraudsters.

Stick said so much in the webinar I mentioned in an earlier chapter. That March 2012 webinar was sponsored by the National Conference of State Legislatures and called "Containing Medicaid Costs: State Strategies to Fight Medicaid Fraud and Abuse."

In relation to Medicaid orthodontic claims in Texas, Stick said: "We have adopted an aggressive approach to credible allegations of fraud. We will now place a credible allegation of fraud hold on a vendor at the intake phase. Normally we would wait until we really got into a case and conducted a good chunk of a full-scale investigation before making a fraud determination. We stopped doing that ...

"So in Texas, we have had problems with orthodontists and dentists abusing the system. So we identified the top fifty utilizers. Identified about $400 million in overpayments and conducted a series—actually, we are in the middle of conducting a series of investigations on those providers."

Stick's antics put some good people out of business, particularly those whose income came almost entirely from Medicaid orthodontic patients, like Dr. Carlos Navarro.

Carlos had eleven clinics totally dedicated to Medicaid orthodontics across the state. He was the state's largest biller and was paid some $22 million in 2010. When the allegations of Medicaid fraud hit, all but one of his clinics closed and he was forced into bankruptcy. Both the state and federal government investigated him criminally for several years but eventually dropped the investigations as they couldn't find any evidence of wrongdoing.

Carlos is an exceptional orthodontist who holds some twenty patents and was treating over 125,000 Medicaid kids with the best state-of-the-art orthodontic care.

The last time I spoke with him, he had two clinics and was no longer treating Medicaid children. His focus is on private-pay patients and he is doing well again. A few years ago, he was pretty dispirited over his fight with the government.

His loss is unfortunate for Medicaid kids. Carlos is a tremendous person and a gifted dentist and businessman. His clinics had an excellent reputation for quality.

This kind of treatment by the government is not limited to Texas. The same thing happened to a very successful Medicaid dentist in New York, Dr. Leonard Morse.

Back in 2013, Dr. Morse was awarded $7.7 million by a New York jury after he had filed suit against the state for falsely accusing him of Medicaid fraud. In 2006 Morse was accused of more than $1 million in fraud by New York state investigators. The New York attorney general at the time had been accused of being "soft" on Medicaid fraud so his investigators were looking for high profile cases to take to the media.

Morse was, at the time, one of the largest billers in the state who served some 30,000 patients, 95 percent of whom were Medicaid patients. Morse was originally arrested on fraud charges and briefly jailed.

However, the case against him was so specious that it was eventually dropped because state investigators could only prove $3,000 in questionable billings.

Morse consequently sued the state in 2011 for $75 million as he had lost not only his multi-million-dollar practice in Brooklyn, but his hospital teaching job and his home as well.

He won the suit because documents from the state showed that investigators had deliberately manipulated information to leave out pertinent facts in order to make it appear that Morse had committed fraud.

Although the award was appealed by the state, the jury verdict was upheld in September 2015.

Why does this happen to good healthcare providers who are successful?

It is very simple. Providers who build their practices on Medicaid and are successful are considered "outliers."

"Outlier" is a statistical term. It basically means a person or thing that is higher or lower than the majority of other people or things being quantified. You know, the bottom or the top of a bell curve. In high school, outliers were both the brainiacs and the guys who couldn't rub two sticks together. Everyone else was in the middle.

So in Medicaid, both high and low performers can be considered outliers.

Government agencies aren't interested in low performers since they are not making any money. But high performers do. As Jack Stick told that webinar back in 2012:

"We determined that at least in this division, the enforcement division, we were a little bit lopsided ... the overwhelming majority of the staff and financial resources were dedicated to recipient investigations. And of course, that is just not really *where the money is* [emphasis added]. So we made a conscious decision that we were going to reevaluate our priorities and that *we were going to go where the money is* [emphasis added]."

Now, that is not too bad because a fraudster could be making a lot of money. But the problem is that rogue bureaucrats like Jack Stick and his ilk can't tell the difference between a fraudster and a competent provider.

A high-performing provider is unfortunately looked at with contempt by bureaucrats since, from a bureaucratic viewpoint, no one can be successful doing Medicaid unless the provider is committing fraud, waste, or abuse. Government officials seem to have no concept of efficiency, competence, or a strong work ethic.

Another example of this happened to a colleague of mine, Dr. Gary Schwarz, a gifted and talented oral surgeon who started his practice in the Rio Grande Valley around 1983, the same time as I did.

With great communication skills and care for his patients, Gary became a well-respected and admired oral surgeon in his community. He developed a very successful practice with many loyal patients and, even though he had great success, he never stopped treating the indigent children in the area.

Gary became a great leader in the Rio Grande Valley Dental Society because he also took the time to be a mentor and educator to his colleagues.

Who would have thought that the government would come after him for defrauding the Medicaid system?

But it did happen. A disgruntled former employee turned on him and became a whistleblower, making false allegations. Gary was arrested and his computers were confiscated by the FBI.

He eventually went to trial and spent hundreds of thousands of dollars in his own defense.

After an eight-day trial, a US District Court jury found Gary innocent of conspiracy and seven counts of Medicaid fraud.

During the trial, it was revealed that federal investigators had paid an informant $10,000 to pose as an intern in Gary's office and shoot undercover video of him working on patients.

This chicanery backfired on the prosecutors. The videos showed a very competent doctor doing oral surgery in a very professional and expedient matter. If I ever need a wisdom tooth extracted, I sure would prefer a five-minute procedure versus an hour-long one.

The worst part for Gary is that he didn't ever need to treat Medicaid children. During the time the government barred him from seeing Medicaid kids, he became the number one implantologist in the state through his private-pay patient base; he didn't need to do Medicaid.

Talk about fraud, waste, and abuse: his whole case was a waste of our tax dollars, which were used simply to try to take out a great Medicaid healthcare provider—a guy who really cares about the indigent children in his home area.

Today, Gary is still treating Medicaid children and serving as president of Dentists Who Care, a charitable organization founded by local dentists. In 2015, he was the number one provider of *pro bono* work for kids and adults who did not have the means to pay for their dental work.

Dr. Gary Schwartz is a hero to many healthcare providers for standing up for his rights and winning the battle.

It is a terrible thing that he had to go through in the first place, but this kind of thing has been going on for years. Even some Texas politicians have firsthand experience with such things and have brought it up in public hearings.

A great example is that of Representative Garnett Coleman from Houston, a member of the House Public Health Committee. Back in 2012, he told in a public hearing about his father who was a Medicaid provider:

"In a world which is more becoming where somebody is considered guilty before innocent, what we don't want in our program with our providers is that they are considered crooks before they are considered good providers of service to the people of the State of Texas. And when you start using a law enforcement model, unfortunately, today people are profiled.

"My father was a Medicaid provider. They put him in the newspaper because he just happened to be serving the women who were poor in the area where we lived. And because he wanted to serve them, he thought it was important that they had good obstetrics and gynecology services. He was put in the newspaper because he actually made some money out of it. But the deal was that he was actually a good doctor and they chose him. See that's the deal and I just don't want to see that we go down a road of immediately considering somebody a crook because they do a lot of the service."

Coleman was talking in a hearing about dentists and the allegations of fraud in Medicaid orthodontic billing. He wanted to try to impress upon the executives of the Health and Human Services Commission in attendance, including then Inspector General Doug Wilson, that they needed to be able to tell the difference between someone being productive and someone committing fraud.

He said, "I'm just asking you to remember that these are small businesses. There are people who, I'll say, game the system and quite frankly steal and those folks should be put into jail and we do that. But in terms of those, you know, who have in good faith, moved forward to try to provide the service,

I just hope as we go through this, that we are careful about separating the wheat from the chaff."

State Senator Royce West from Dallas at another hearing told these executives the same thing: "What we don't want to see; we need to do this, don't get me wrong, but those individuals who have been providing care, Medicaid dentists, I sure don't want to see us run them out. Then we end up having a shortage of individuals that people can go to. We need to be real sensitive."

Naturally, they weren't.

CHAPTER 9

ROGUE GOVERNMENT AGENCIES

Unfortunately for taxpayers, very often government boondoggles continue to occur with little effective action being taken.

The Texas Health and Human Services Commission is a prime example because, over the last ten or so years, there has been one multi-million-dollar disaster for taxpayers after another.

One example started back in January 2006 when HHSC Executive Commissioner Albert Hawkins prematurely launched a new privatized system to screen and enroll low-income families into government programs.

The $893 million project, the largest privatization scheme in state history at that time, massively flopped. Four privately-run call centers were to take over and eliminate the need for several thousand government employees and a number of government offices around the state. The plan was touted to be a private sector miracle to save the taxpayers of Texas some $600 million.

However, within twenty months, the contract was canceled and the situation ended up costing tens of millions to fix, not to mention outraging Texans and the federal government.

Hawkins blamed the private contractor Accenture. He said he was given assurances that they were ready to proceed. Yet, the company said it told Hawkins it wasn't ready—that there were problems that needed to be fixed before the system could launch. Hawkins didn't listen. It cost the state $30 million.

While legislative committees held hearings afterward to try to get to the root of the problem, the best they could come up with was that Hawkins was impatient and pushed the project forward when he shouldn't have. The result: Hawkins was re-appointed to his position by Governor Rick Perry.

That result doesn't make sense, does it? Yet, it makes sense if you realize most of the time governments don't want to get to the bottom of why things are going wrong.

How do I know?

A couple of years ago, we found out about a company called Reflective Medical.

Prior to all the media uproar in 2011 about the dollars Texas was spending on braces for Medicaid children, apparently, the Governor's Office had become concerned about conditions at HHSC.

This company, Reflective Medical, from California, was in Austin to discuss opportunities for providing electronic health record services to the state. It was early 2010.

During the course of a meeting with staff from the Governor's Office about this, one of the staff asked Dr. David Gibson, the CEO of the company, if they had any experience with Medicaid fraud. Gibson answered in the affirmative. His company had on its board a number of retired, highly decorated government employees and FBI agents who had cut their teeth digging up fraud in the Medicaid system in California.

These individuals included Gibson himself; Alan Cates, who established the California Medical Fraud Prevention Bureau; Ed O'Donnell, a retired FBI special agent and recipient of the FBI Director's Award for healthcare fraud investigation; and James Weddick, another recipient of the FBI Director's Award and former member of the FBI's corruption squad in Sacramento, which prosecuted five California lawmakers on racketeering and corruption charges in the 1990s.

They were asked to look in at HHSC and find out what was going on and report back.

Initially, Gibson and crew had great cooperation from executives and staff at HHSC. They were able to look at three years' worth of Texas Medicaid data and analyze it using their proprietary fraud detection software. In fact, they made it into a "proof of concept" for the state.

However, what they found soon soured the relationship.

They expected to find accurate eligibility files for Medicaid beneficiaries, which are the core requirement for preventing fraud. But that wasn't the case.

Instead they found that the HHSC couldn't track which Texans were eligible for services under Medicaid, where they lived, their genders, or their medical conditions. They could find no evidence that HHSC even checked public records to determine if a beneficiary was alive or dead at the time of service.

Gibson knew the unreliability of the demographic data in the eligibility files provided an open portal for thieves to access the program's funding and bill for services never rendered.

Out of the total number of member records reviewed, about six million were found to be missing address information (blank addresses were provided). Anyone could bill for them.

In fact, they found that in the three years of Medicaid data they reviewed, there were forty-eight eligible Medicaid beneficiaries over the age of 115. These ranged in age from 116 to a high of 196.

They also found 11,641 Medicaid beneficiaries to have a recorded age above 99 years.

Pretty unlikely!

They also found that the Medicaid program was paying for male procedures on females, such as the removal of the testes, circumcision, biopsy of the prostate, etc., and for treating girls under ten years of age for vaginal prolapse, care after delivery, dilation of vagina, etc.

They were also paying for female procedures performed on males, such as biopsy of the uterine lining, care after delivery, care of miscarriage, etc.

The state also paid 101 Medicaid claims for pregnancy-related procedures that were performed on males.

Wow, what a travesty!

Gibson and his group identified 6,470 suspect vendors. But they were informed by HHSC that HHSC already had a list of some 8,000 known or suspected fraudulent providers that included their list of targets.

Unbelievably, they found that HHSC was still paying these suspect providers and had paid out $103.9 million to them between 2008 and January 2010 and continued to pay them.

Gibson and his team were shocked.

Worse, they could not determine what criteria was used by HHSC to include the 8,000 individuals and businesses on their list and why investigations were not initiated when there were apparently credible indications for contracted providers being included on the target list.

Gibson advised HHSC senior management that "a viable Medicaid program, managed by competent officials, would have immediately suspended all payments to those targeted providers and prioritized their investigations and prosecutions to eliminate the continued hemorrhaging of public funds."

The honeymoon was over for Reflective Medical.

"Initially, we had great cooperation from the HHSC staff," Gibson told media. "But as we uncovered more and more evidence of inadequate program-administrative oversight, tempers started to flare at the senior management level and our welcome wore thin. Senior management's threat to sue our company if we ever revealed the contents of our report to the legislature or the governor's office was the final development that ended our interest in Texas. You simply cannot help an organization that actively resists assistance. I believe no one wanted to take responsibility for how bad the problems were at HHSC. Candidly, we were surprised how bad it was too."

Despite this animosity, Gibson offered to give the Health and Human Services Commission Office of Inspector General free use of the Reflective Medical's advanced proprietary software to uncover Medicaid fraud.

However, after delivery of their final report in the spring of 2011, Gibson and his crew were unceremoniously terminated and again warned sternly that if they breathed a word about the contents of their report to anyone, they would be considered in breach of the confidentiality agreement in their "proof of concept" contract and sued by the Texas Attorney General.

They hadn't received a cent for their work because they did it *pro bono*.

They took that warning about a lawsuit to heart until late 2014.

At that time, HHSC, trying to come clean with the media and public in the wake of the 21CT contracting scandal for Medicaid fraud detection software I mentioned earlier, revealed that Reflective Medical and three other firms had submitted "proofs of concept" for their software.

Gibson's comments to the media didn't make much of a splash as their report was already a few years old and unfortunately now paled in comparison to the media storm surrounding HHSC and its executives shepherding multi-million-dollar state contracts to their friends in violation of state contracting laws.

David Gibson is bitter about his Texas experience. In fact, he is bitter about his experience with other states and federal government agencies too.

He had written to Dr. Shantanu Agrawal, Deputy Administrator and Director of the Center for Program Integrity at the Centers for Medicare & Medicaid Services with a copy to Senator Orrin Hatch about how easy it would be to change the Medicaid system to reduce fraud. He outlined it plainly because he knows how it can be done. His letter was in response to a plea that Agrawal had made in an interview with the *New York Times* that he wanted public input on how to stop Medicaid fraud because he didn't know how.

Gibson didn't even receive the courtesy of a reply. He thinks government agency concern about Medicaid fraud is a joke, that there is little sincerity about doing something effective about it.

The lesson here is that it is up to us, the taxpayers, to keep our government agencies honest.

We have to fight back and make the system run right.

That's what I did and it was effective.

CHAPTER 10
FIGHTING BACK

I have already told you that we won our court battles. I really had thought this situation would go away after our initial court victory at the beginning of 2012 but it only got worse. It was almost like we never went to court to begin with.

The state, instead of backing off, came on stronger and they were pretty unrepentant about attempting to label me a criminal to try to get back money that had already gone to necessary treatment for Medicaid children. The state, after all, had approved every case before we began treatment.

When I went to court to force them to release the funds they had withheld by payment hold, the OIG lawyer actually argued that the state did not have to reimburse monies improperly collected from anyone even if the state was totally wrong! It was ludicrous. Their strategy seemed to be to make me spend more money on legal fees so I would become amenable to settling for what they wanted or force me into bankruptcy.

So this told me that I was dealing with more than a legal case. There had to be political pressures driving this. I was at a loss.

Fortunately, I received some excellent help beyond just legal advice.

You have to understand I was pretty much on my own. Because of all the negative media that had run about dentists supposedly ripping off Medicaid, dentists were running for cover. Even colleagues I had known for many years didn't know what to think and were fearful of supporting someone in apparent trouble with the government on so sensitive an issue. Even those also accused, but felt they had done nothing wrong, were fearful. They hadn't studied and practiced for years to become dentists to now deal with such incredible issues.

The Texas Dental Association was not helpful. Only around 10 percent of their membership is involved with Medicaid, so it's not a big issue for them. In fact, there was a rumor that the investigative reporter for WFAA, Byron Harris, was tipped off to the large amount of Medicaid spending on braces by a past executive member of the TDA. The individual did so because of professional jealousy of a Medicaid dentist who was extremely successful.

There was another rumor that the media was tipped off by a Dallas law firm that was looking to specialize in personal injury and *qui tam* dental cases. (A *qui tam* lawsuit is one that rewards whistleblowers if their cases recover funds for the government.)

Whatever the truth is, I don't know, and it actually doesn't really matter.

To help me with this situation, I initiated some personal actions that were successful.

First, I took a sabbatical from my dental practice and spent time visiting my church and getting pastoral counseling. Religion can be a great comfort no matter what your faith. For me, it was a great support and helped me maintain a highly ethical mindset during this whole time of upset. The counseling I received gave me the strength and ability to continue to stand up to the state and their allegations, continuing to know, despite massive pressure otherwise, that we had not done anything wrong.

After all, we were successful as one of the largest dental practices in Texas. Our practice had twenty-eight years of continuous growth until this payment hold situation erupted. Our success was all done through a tremendous amount of hard work, training, and continuing education. I had trained as a management consultant at the Hubbard College of Administration in Los Angeles where I learned workable business principles to steer my office in the right direction for expansion. Fraud had no place in our organization. What honest healthcare professional would risk his whole career for any amount of ill-gotten gain?

Being a very spiritual person has kept me sane through this whole ordeal and has helped me to keep improving conditions in my sphere of influence, which now includes HHSC and OIG.

The next thing I did was solicit the help of Dr. Tom Orent, who is a great opinion leader in dentistry. Having experienced the ups and downs of running a dental practice himself, he built a consulting company to help dental practices put in systems to improve their bottom line through the Internet, telephone, and mastermind meetings. The GEMGroup, as they are known, focuses on clinical and team-building technology that helps practices provide optimal care to patients. It was not long after I started attending these meetings that I expanded my practice to six additional satellite offices. This got us back on track as an expanding dental practice.

Some very good help also came from a marketing company that I had just hired at the beginning of 2012 to help market my dental practice online. I knew the owner, George Mentis, of Target Public Marketing out of Austin and we spoke several times about the Medicaid issue just as a matter of interest. In fact, one morning we started the conversation over an early breakfast at the IHOP in Harlingen.

George, who had also been involved in PR work, checked around with several of his colleagues and several media people he knew and the word on the street was that I was doomed because everyone believed implicitly that all the dentists were guilty. The reputation of OIG was such that an allegation was as good as guilt.

What a horrible situation!

George told me that unless there was some proof or documentation countering the allegations, there was little that could be done, reputation-wise, other than put a good face on the situation and not bring it up unless asked about it.

This all changed when we obtained the transcripts of my hearing from April.

George now had a colleague who was doing work for him, Al Anthony, who had lots of experience in public relations, review the situation. We all met again for breakfast at the

IHOP. We discussed the fact that we now needed to tell my story and take the matter to Texas politicians as clearly the OIG bureaucrats were out of control.

I really didn't think this would be effective because a number of key politicians, such as State Senator Jane Nelson, had been in the media condemning all dentists who were being targeted with the allegations of fraud.

Al told me that they only knew what the bureaucrats and media had been telling them. They had no idea what was really happening. I found that hard to believe.

However, almost as soon as he had finished talking about this, who should walk into the IHOP? It was State Senator Eddie Lucio Jr. of Brownsville. He was obviously coming in for his own breakfast meeting and sat down with a group of businessmen.

We looked around the table at each other—what a coincidence!

I was reluctant but both George and Al counseled that this was a golden opportunity to arrange a meeting with Lucio. I had met with him previously and developed a good rapport with him. There it was—an opportunity to do something to help Medicaid providers. I got up and introduced myself to him and obtained his agreement to meet. Our campaign to fix this situation had begun.

And it was true. George and Al were right. The politicians didn't know what was going on. So I made it my business to inform them.

We put together a fifty-two-page briefing pack that told the story of what had happened with this investigation into my dental practice. It contained my background, how successful my practice had become, and my community involvement and then explained about the injustice of the actions of OIG with pertinent documents to prove what we wrote. It contained very graphic pictures of the teeth of a number of the children we had treated that the state now said shouldn't have qualified for Medicaid. They are pretty hard to look at. I used this pack in my meetings.

I initially met with Senator Lucio in July 2012 and he provided me with an invitation letter to meet with others. I had numerous meetings at the end of July with assistants from Senator Carlos Uresti, Senator Judith Zaffarini, Senator Royce West, Senator Jane Nelson, Senator Bob Deull, House Representative Lois Kolkhorst, and Representative Garnet Coleman.

I did end up meeting with a number of the politicians themselves as well as quite a few more assistants. Several individuals realized that something was dreadfully wrong with what was happening and became champions for Medicaid dentists. Among them were Representative Bobby Guerra; Senator Juan "Chuy" Hinojosa, both from McAllen; and Representative Richard Peña Raymond of Laredo. They saw the injustice of what was going on. More about them later.

Although I was now meeting with politicians, the initial headway was not great.

So again, I met with George and Al and it was determined that we needed to start a group around this issue of Medicaid provider rights and get support. So we started that too.

In August of 2012, there was the annual two-day *Dentists Who Care* Charity Conference on South Padre Island. *Dentists Who Care* is a wonderfully innovative program sponsored by the dentists of the Rio Grande Valley. They fund a mobile dental clinic and offer a voucher system to provide dental treatment for poor children in the area who don't qualify for Medicaid or other insurance. More than 16,000 children have been helped and $6.8 million in charitable dental care has been provided by over 200 dentist volunteers through the mobile dental unit and voucher system since 1999.

During the conference, George and Al conducted a survey of the dentists who attended, both those who took Medicaid and those that didn't. They wanted to see what concerns they had and if they would support a group. The survey gave some interesting results.

For example, they found that the 60 percent of dentists who took Medicaid had a bleak outlook on the future of dentistry in Texas. But 100 percent of those who did not take Medicaid were optimistic about the future—a huge difference in attitude. The state investigations into Medicaid orthodontic treatment and other difficulties with Medicaid—the low reimbursement rates, red tape with billing and procedures, etc.—were depressing those involved in the program.

However, when Medicaid dentists were asked about their motivation for taking Medicaid, almost every dentist replied that it was to help children and their families. They had taken on Medicaid for altruistic reasons. It was their altruism that kept them involved despite the problems it created for them.

It was a sad finding that those who wanted to help others and give back to the community were being punished for it rather than rewarded. Dentists not involved in Medicaid were far happier and had fewer concerns.

The good news was that when these dentists were asked what was needed to improve the situation, they said a strong association representing the interests of dentists, lobbying/legislation in favor of dentists, and Medicaid reform could help fix the system.

We also found out at this conference on South Padre that the Texas Dental Association definitely was not going to help us.

TDA President Michael Stewart had attended our town hall meeting with the assembled dentists from the Valley. Several of us asked him what the TDA was going to do to help the dentists such as myself who had been accused of fraud but were innocent. He didn't mince his words. He told everyone he was offended that anyone would bring the matter up as the TDA did not support fraud. He apparently had already made up his mind that everyone was guilty.

These factors led to my forming *Texas Dentists for Medicaid Reform,* which began when its website went live in December of 2012.

This is from the About Section on the website at www.tdmr.org:

"Texas Dentists for Medicaid Reform is organized by dentists who are concerned about the future of dental care for the over three million Texas children eligible for Medicaid.

"Their practices, their reputations, and their families have been hurt by the bureaucratic red-tape and bungling of state Medicaid officials and the unjust tactics of their enforcement arm, the Office of Inspector General ...

"95 percent of dentists surveyed who take Medicaid patients do so for altruistic reasons—helping impoverished children and families obtain needed dental care. When they are successful and honest, they deserve to be assisted and protected for their efforts. They should not be savaged by a system, that as it currently is, only treats them as criminals.

"That is why the Texas Dentists for Medicaid Reform was created."

We've had a lot of excellent people become involved with us as staff and on the board.

Gregory Ewing, a Washington DC healthcare lawyer with extensive compliance experience, became our president and continues to serve in that role to this day.

Dr. Tara Rios, former House Representative from Brownsville who also had a tragic involvement with false allegations of Medicaid fraud a number of years ago, joined our board along with myself and Dr. Vivian Teegardin, my partner at Harlingen Family Dentistry.

Richard Garza, a healthcare executive involved with the Texas Association of Rural Health Clinics, was an early staff member along with Lorie Imken, who was our office manager in Austin through a very hectic first legislative session in 2013. She set up a number of dinner briefings around the state for dentists about TDMR.

Ernest Pedraza, a childhood friend from Harlingen who retired as a commander from the Austin police department, helped with research for TDMR.

In that first legislative session, Hugo Berlanga, a well-known and well-liked former member of the state house, now a lobbyist, ably assisted us with our agenda to get due process rights for Medicaid providers.

Mark Vane, an attorney and lobbyist, has since been instrumental helping us reach politicians of both stripes on Medicaid reform issues along with Dr. Chad Evans of Smile Magic and his group, *Dental Association for Underserved Children*.

Another key player has been Chuck Young, who helped us as a talented researcher and as a spokesperson that first year. He did some excellent work. Chuck had founded *Texans for Accountable Government* (TAG), a non-partisan political action committee headquartered in Austin.

Those are the players.

So now let me tell you about what we did and accomplished to help change the game.

CHAPTER 11
TURNING THE TIDE

It wasn't easy at the beginning.

It was pretty lonely and it was getting expensive with legal fees, but there was nothing else to do but to continue on.

So this is where the Texas Dentists for Medicaid Reform really came in. With the website we set up, starting in December of 2012, we could not only tell our own story but the story of other dentists and what was occurring with each case. I wanted to see real due process rights for all Medicaid providers.

Our first story, published on December 10, 2012, was "Harlingen Family Dentistry Wins Major, Precedent-Setting Decision in Texas Medicaid Orthodontics Case."

Then we started publishing relevant stories such as:

"Political Fact-Checking Website Slam Against Statistical Claims on Texas Medicaid Orthodontia Spending Heralded by Texas Dentists for Medicaid Reform,"

"Survey of Texas Dentists Shows Deep Dissatisfaction with Medicaid,"

"TDMR Submits Written Testimony to the Texas Senate Finance Committee on Lack of Due Process for Medicaid Providers,"

"State Office of Inspector General Drops Case Against Ortho Dentist,"

"Will Texas Be Held Legally Liable By Dentists Falsely Accused of Medicaid Fraud – As New York State Has Been?" and

"Texas Valley Dental Society Announces Endorsement of the Texas Dentists for Medicaid Reform."

We had a fax list for all relevant senators and house representatives at the Austin Capitol, an e-mail list to all dental Medicaid providers we obtained through an open records request, plus we started to have interested individuals subscribe to our "TDMR News Alerts."

It started small but it became a very effective strategy, coupled with meetings with our elected officials and testifying before legislative committees.

In late 2012, Representative Bobby Guerra met with me several times along with other dentists and agreed to bring forward legislation to ensure Medicaid providers had due process rights. He drafted, with help from my lawyer Tony Canales, House Bill 1536, which was filed in the spring 2013 session of the Texas Legislature. It was a bill to add due process rights for Medicaid providers into legislation. The great thing about the bill was that it would allow a Medicaid provider to get a trial before a district court if they disagreed with previous administrative court rulings. It is, after all, a constitutional right to get a trial before one's peers.

As the session started in January, George Mentis and Chuck Young went traveling around the state holding dinner meetings for concerned dentists. They went to Houston, Dallas, San Antonio, and El Paso as well as other cities.

Our activity was getting us noticed. As fraudsters tend to run and hide, the fact that we were meeting with our elected representatives, pushing pro-active legislation, standing up in front of legislative committees, and holding meetings around the state was building us a credible presence.

In fact, we were getting noticed so much that when we held a meeting at the Omni Southpark Hotel in Austin for dentists at the end of February, WFAA reporter Byron Harris decided to show up. The meeting was private, so he did not come in, but I spent half an hour in an interview with him telling him about TDMR and what we were doing.

Of course, when the story actually aired at the beginning of March, the spin was negative, although Harris, during the course of our time together, agreed that my practice had gotten a bad rap after having won our administrative hearing. As Harris had long ago committed to the fraud angle with his reporting, the story's spin was not hard to understand since he was given a number of press awards for his reporting on this issue. This became quite obvious because at one legislative hearing we attended, he was there with his cameras but did not bother to report on the dramatic testimony being given by dentists who were adversely affected by the Office of Inspector General and by Jack Stick.

As other press started to tell the dentists' side of the story, Harris and WFAA became silent on orthodontic Medicaid fraud. Harris, after a long and illustrious career, retired in 2014.

TDMR and a number of dentists participated in a hearing before the House Human Services Committee on the due process bill, HB 1536.

Dr. Tara Rios DDS, former House Representative and TDMR board member, sent written testimony in which she told the committee that "I was indicted by the United States Attorney General's Office and the Attorney General of Texas on serious anti-kickback violations in 2010. All charges were subsequently dismissed in Federal Court by a United States District Judge.

"During this incident, I saw first-hand the overzealous and overreaching actions of the Attorney General of Texas Office and the United States Office of Attorney General. Prior to the indictment, a Texas MFCU (Medicaid Fraud Control Unit) agent called to inquire about a visit, I attempted to set up a meeting to answer questions they may have. When the Texas state agents learned I would have my attorney present, I was informed by state agents they would cancel the appointment if my attorney was present during this meeting. The meeting was canceled by the MFCU agents. This is one example of the gaming of a system to create fear and mistrust by all parties."

The most electric testimony came from Dr. Paul Dunn. Paul is an old-time country dentist from Levelland, sixty-seven years old. The actions of OIG had placed his practice and professional life at risk.

Paul told the committee and wrote in his written testimony: "On January 2, 2013, I received a registered letter from HHSC stating they had found three examples of possible fraud out of the 70 patients [cases HHSC-OIG reviewed] and were placing a hold on all Medicaid funds. My practice is 90% Medicaid and that basically shut down all cash flow to my practice ... [In a meeting] Mr. Stick [OIG Deputy Inspector General for Enforcement] told me that he didn't see any evidence of fraud. But he then indicated that OIG wanted 40% of my income back from the time that I had been working with the Medicaid program. Mr. Stick told me that if I wrote a check to OIG for $1.2 million then this might all go away. If I sold everything I own with my life insurance thrown in, I couldn't raise $1.2 million."

The electricity entered the hearing because Jack Stick happened to be there, representing his agency. Stick faced a grueling thirty minutes of questioning from committee members—Chairman Richard Peña Raymond, Representative John Zerwas, a physician, and Representative Pat Fallon.

He had to face comments like the following from Chairman Raymond:

"But can you understand the concept, certainly it bothers me, that we're giving a state agency the authority to bankrupt businesses. To bankrupt people who are doctors and without ever having to go to, without having their day in court. Can you do that? Do you understand that concept and the concern there?"

It was the first time the chinks in the armor of Stick's agency were being shown. Stick and his boss, Doug Wilson, for months had been telling other legislative committees about the dire amount of Medicaid dental fraud and how they needed money to buy new software and increase staff to deal with it.

Stick had even told the House Appropriations Committee that Texas would escape any need to repay the federal government any Medicaid funds from the orthodontic billings he alleged were fraudulent if dentists went bankrupt.

There was further success when the influential Senator Jane Nelson, who had publicly spoken out about the alleged orthodontic Medicaid fraud and dentists who had "gamed" the system, decided to back due process rights for providers. This was after a hearing of the Senate Health and Human Services Committee of which she was the chair. TDMR had testified before the committee.

Senator Nelson asked Senator Joan Huffman to draft a bill which eventually became Senate Bill 1803. Unfortunately, in the give and take of getting a bill to pass, the provision for a trial before a district court was not included and a provision for making providers pay half the cost of their administrative hearings was included. But the bill, which took the place of HB 1536, for the first time, enshrined in legislation due process rights for administrative actions against providers. That was fantastic progress.

The bill passed both the Texas Senate and House unanimously and was signed into law by Governor Rick Perry in June 2013.

The Texas Medical Association and the Texas Hospital Association had also backed the bill. It was a great victory for Medicaid providers—or so we thought.

Later in the year, after the bill came into force September 1, we found that OIG was using the provision to have Medicaid providers pay half of their administrative hearing costs to try to collect huge amounts of money up front that prevented providers from even getting to court. This meant a provider already under a payment hold and hard-pressed financially would be required to pay, up front, anywhere from ten to twenty thousand dollars to get to court. It barred the way for many. It is diabolical how an agency can twist things to make a situation even worse.

It just showed the agency was in severe need of reform. Its day would come.

In May 2013, Dr. Behzad Nazari became the second dentist in Texas to come before an administrative court on allegations of Medicaid orthodontic fraud. It was over a year after my case had been heard.

Because of all the contention with my case, the State Office of Administrative Hearings had two judges assigned to hear Dr. Nazari's case.

And the state, because it had been beaten up so badly in my decision, paid $250,000 to several outside lawyers—James Moriarty and Dan Hargrove—to plead their case before the judges. Moriarty and Hargrove are *qui tam* attorneys who seek whistleblowers to provide evidence of fraud and misconduct against dentists.

The hearing lasted four days but the decision didn't come out until that November. The judges totally exonerated Dr. Nazari and his Houston clinic, Antoine Dental Center, from allegations of Medicaid fraud and excoriated the state's case and expert witnesses against him.

Another blow to the state.

Slowly but surely, the media environment started to change too. There was a creeping doubt that perhaps the state wasn't being totally honest about the allegations of vast Medicaid fraud by Texas dentists.

An indicator that the tides were changing was a feature article published in the *San Antonio Express* in September. It was the first media piece telling the dentists' side of the story.

Titled "In Medicaid, docs guilty until proven innocent," reporter Jeremy Roebuck reviewed the state's allegations of fraud and found them wanting. I was featured in the article and spoke about what had happened to my practice and my life.

Senator Juan "Chuy" Hinojosa was quoted. He told the *Express* that: "There's no doubt that there's fraud taking place across the state. But that doesn't mean you can wage a total war on providers, take down innocent businesses and ruin reputations. That's not the way justice works."

Lawyer David DeGroot, who had represented providers in negotiations with OIG, told the paper that providers would have to settle rather than carry on costly litigation.

He said, "It's like a shakedown. The OIG never has to prove its case, and generally, providers can't afford to fight it. They fold — they either pay up or just stop treating Medicaid patients."

The truth was getting out there!

CHAPTER 12

THE STATE STRIKES BACK

The state had suffered its greatest defeat at the hands of the dentists much like when the rebel alliance in *Star Wars* destroyed the Empire's greatest weapon, the Death Star. And just like the Empire, the state did strike back.

It was pretty underhanded, too, although there were earlier glimpses of such tactics when OIG had started a new investigation into my practice when they had lost the administrative court decision.

This was a whole new order of trouble. Keep in mind that an administrative decision made in the case of any Medicaid provider had to be approved by the Health and Human Services Commission itself. This gave the Commission the power to overturn administrative court decisions it didn't like. This is like the prosecution in a criminal trial being able to overturn a jury decision of innocence in any case.

In my case back in 2012, their own judge, Susan Fekety in the HHSC Appeals Court, had turned against them and upheld the decision of the administrative court judge and then had retired immediately afterward. We had heard rumors from former and current employees of OIG about pressure within the agency. The OIG was having a large turnover of staff due to Jack Stick's apparently despotic management style.

This type of behavior apparently could not be borne a second time with the Nazari decision. The fix had to go in and so it did.

A new HHSC judge, Rick Gilpin, who used to work for the Office of the Attorney General, the agency responsible for prosecuting the Nazari's case for OIG, overturned the decision. He rewrote the administrative court decision, simply cutting and pasting directly from the state's case documents into his own.

This turn with Gilpin was extremely bizarre. So bizarre that Nazari's lawyers filed a motion that Gilpin should recuse himself because of his former association with the prosecution of the case.

More bizarre is that they had to file the motion with the HHSC Appeals Court itself. Worse, the Office of Attorney General, which opposed the motion, wrote in their own pleadings that such conflict of interest laws didn't apply because HHSC Appeals Court judges aren't "real judges." Huh?

Not surprisingly, keeping true to the kangaroo nature of the court, one of Gilpin's fellows simply denied the motion with no comment whatsoever.

However, the real dirty work came in May 2014 when the then Executive Commissioner of HHSC Kyle Janek issued his final decision in the Nazari case based on Gilpin's earlier ruling.

As Jack Stick had been promoted to HHSC Chief Counsel earlier, it undoubtedly had his stamp upon it.

Janek's ruling went beyond just overturning the detailed ruling of the two administrative judges who had heard four days of testimony on Nazari's case and found no evidence of Medicaid fraud. Janek not only found Nazari and his clinic culpable of Medicaid fraud and maintained in place his payment hold, he went further and rewrote my earlier favorable decision.

Janek wrote in his ruling that he found "certain of the findings in the Harlingen Family Dental case incorrectly stated the law, rules, and Medicaid policy and cannot be relied on in this case."

Wow. My lawyer Jason Ray couldn't believe it. It threw everything into turmoil. Nazari was forced to appeal and spend money he no longer had. I didn't know what was going to happen in my case.

It looked like the Office of the Attorney General and the Health and Human Services Commission had rigged things so they couldn't lose.

It was a pretty bleak moment!

The state was still withholding at that time some $1.5 million that we had earned. Legal expenses were getting heavier. While I had been able to reduce our office's dependency on Medicaid patients, it was still tough going getting new patients.

Settlement wasn't an option. Why would I pay the state some $2.7 million when I hadn't done anything wrong? Of course, such a settlement would include a statement that there was no admission of wrongdoing on our part but it was too high a cost of doing business and such a settlement would be wrong.

Many business people feel getting the state off your back with such a settlement is a cost of doing business. The problem is that people, no matter what the agreement says, will view the settlement as an admission of guilt, not to mention that it's basically extortion.

It's against my nature to give into something like that.

So I resolved to carry on to the bitter end. And I resolved to expand, not contract like so many other dentists had done. I looked for opportunities to add to my practice and found them.

As time went along, I found a dentist in Brownsville who was retiring and bought out his practice. I found a location in Edinburg that I liked and put an office in there. In Raymondville, I built an entirely new building with state-of-the-art facilities that is now operating and serving the needs of the community. I also opened offices in Weslaco and McAllen and I found a partner for an office in northwest Austin.

Instead of bankrupting me or forcing my practice to close, the state government had inspired me to grow and I now have seven offices.

Of course, just as things looked darkest, like a warrior with severe injuries to his arms and legs about to be run over by an enemy tank, I had to find the strength and energy to keep moving.

This whole ordeal kindled my purpose to be an advocate for fair exchanges between government and honest tax payers. I was willing to lose everything I owned for this principle. I found my fortitude and things did begin to change for the better.

CHAPTER 13
CHANGING THE SYSTEM

After Dr. Nazari suffered his loss at the hands of Kyle Janek's decision, it started to look to the press even more like some kind of fix was in.

We had been writing stories on the TDMR website about the fact that *all* orthodontic treatments that dentists had performed for Medicaid had to be pre-approved by the state's Medicaid contractor, the Texas Medicaid and Healthcare Partnership led by Xerox, before *any* work could be done.

We learned that in 2008 the OIG had conducted its own audit of Xerox's orthodontic prior authorization process and reported that it was lax. It turned out the company was using so-called "dental specialists" to review each case. These "specialists" were basically high school graduates who had no dental training whatsoever; they worked from home and were paid on piecework.

Medicaid dentists relied on the TMHP review and approval process to begin any orthodontic treatment of patients and had been led to believe by the state dental director, Dr. Linda Altenhoff, that each treatment application was reviewed by a board-certified orthodontist. She said this at a Medicaid orthodontic stakeholders' meeting held in Austin in January 2009.

So the state, rather than going after this apparent fraud, decided to shake down Texas dentists who were successful in helping indigent children with their oral health.

The shakedown was becoming too apparent and was making the upper echelons of the state government look bad nationally. Especially since those upper echelons were looking to run for the presidency—Governor Rick Perry.

So the first really good thing that happened, like a light at the end of a tunnel, was a two-part exposé published at the beginning of May 2014 by the *Texas Tribune* entitled "Company That OK'd Unnecessary Braces Kept Its Contract."

It was republished in the *New York Times*!

The stories pointed out that while the state was going hammer and tongs after dentists, it was ignoring Xerox's role in the affair. It also happened to detail the political connections between the governor's office and the company.

Within a week of the *New York Times* piece running, the Office of the Attorney General of Texas filed suit against Xerox for Medicaid fraud. At the same time, the Health and Human Services Commission terminated Xerox's contract as the state's Medicaid contractor.

Talk about good news!

I have a rather humorous anecdote about this. At the same time as the *Tribune* published its articles on Xerox's soft treatment by the state, my lawyer, Jason Ray, and I met with Inspector General Doug Wilson to see if we could settle my case.

Wilson had little understanding or sympathy, which enraged me. So I started coming down on him about Xerox and how he had done nothing about the company even though his agency knew for a long time about its bad performance on the orthodontic prior authorizations.

He then said a remarkable thing. He told me that Xerox had nothing to do with it at all and it was all on the providers.

When the news broke a few days later about the state suing Xerox and terminating its contract, I realized how far out of the loop he must have been. He had been living in a vacuum.

As far as the lawsuit against Xerox was concerned, I and another few dentists were elated. We decided to also sue Xerox and the state as well! Unfortunately, this is a slow boat and nothing has really developed yet.

We were starting to feel better; we were finally making headway.

In March 2014, three staff from the Texas Sunset Advisory Commission came to my office. The commission reviews state agencies every five or ten years to see if they are living up to their mandate and recommends changes if needed or dissolution if the agency is found to be unnecessary. The process involves the staff of the commission inspecting the agency then issuing a report with recommendations. Next, public hearings are held before the commission on the report and recommendations, with the commission issuing a final report and recommendations to be adopted as legislation in the upcoming legislative session. The commission is primarily made up of state house representatives and senators.

The commission staff came to my office as HHSC and its OIG were under review and they were going around and interviewing stakeholders about their operation.

I communicated the facts of our ordeal with the OIG. I told them the story about my meeting with Jack Stick and his comment about being able to find a "Medicaid program violation on Jesus Christ." They informed me that they had already heard about that one. Apparently, Stick was quite proud of the remark.

In August, two further things happened that sealed the fate of OIG's sunset review process.

One, the federal Office of Inspector General of the Department of Health released an audit that placed responsibility for the amount of spending on Medicaid orthodontic treatment in Texas squarely on the shoulders of the state government, not the dentists. After all, the state contractor was responsible for approving the treatments and the state wrote the checks, didn't they?

The second incident was incredible.

OIG had been going after Austin dentist Dr. Rachel Trueblood for $16 million in Medicaid overpayments on the basis of allegations of fraud. Dr. Trueblood, who exclusively treated poor, Medicaid-eligible children, had to close her four clinics and set adrift hundreds of patients and all her staff.

The unrelenting demand for a multi-million-dollar settlement from Dr. Trueblood ceased when her lawyers asked

OIG to provide the methodology by which they calculated this $16 million overpayment.

Within a week of the request, OIG offered to settle the entire Trueblood case for $39,000, less than 1% of what they had been demanding and the actual amount of billing discrepancies they allegedly found. Dr. Trueblood, with no admission of wrongdoing, instantly settled for the insanely reduced amount as she had no desire or financial reserves to fight any further legal battle.

OIG blamed the "error" on a department actuary who they said was found to be improperly extrapolating the massive figures and couldn't justify his work. They not only fired him but asked the Texas Rangers to conduct a criminal investigation. As of yet, two years later, no arrests or charges have been laid.

The press had a field day with the settlement, further calling into question the competency and honesty of OIG.

The Sunset Advisory Commission also picked up on the incident. Inspector General Doug Wilson was left reeling during public hearings conducted by the Commission in November.

Why not? He had been telling legislators that his agency had discovered some $1.1 billion in Medicaid provider overpayments for 2012 and 2013, yet they had only collected $5.5 million during that period of time.

Anyway, when the staff report went public in October, it exposed the deception within the agency.

The report said in part:

"The findings and discussion that follow regarding OIG present a rather harsh assessment, borne of a remarkable consistency of feedback from a range of interests and stakeholders and backed by the first-hand observations of Sunset staff, built over 11 months of review work. These conclusions are not made lightly, but are made instead in full recognition of the need for a strong and nimble OIG to ensure the integrity of these critically important HHS programs. No matter how one views the HHS system, it exists to serve a purpose, and the public must have confidence that it works properly. OIG is essential to the effort to instill that confidence.

"OIG has the difficult and crucial job of protecting the integrity of the HHS system and its public assistance programs, including Medicaid. However, OIG's highest profile responsibilities — investigative processes — lack structure, guidelines, and measurement of data needed to analyze and improve its processes and outcomes. Absence of basic tools such as decision-making criteria to guide its investigative work may contribute to inconsistent results and unfair investigative processes. Inefficient and ineffective processes lead to limited outcomes and a modest return on investment to the state. These concerns, taken in sum with other issues such as poor communication and transparency, limited staff training, and a lack of performance data from a case management system, point to limited oversight and the need for further review."

At the public hearings, Doug Wilson faced many stiff questions from Representative Raymond, Senator Hinojosa, and Chairman Jane Nelson, amongst others.

Senator Charles Schwertner, a member of the commission and also Chairman of the Senate Health and Human Services Committee, simply told Wilson that "we have a loss of confidence in your office."

However, there was worse to come for Wilson.

Wilson and Stick's house of cards both came tumbling down almost unexpectedly.

December 2014 was bad for Doug Wilson and HHSC executive commissioner Kyle Janek. It was probably the worst scandal to befall a Texas government agency.

It was caused by Jack Stick.

Here is the short version. It came to the attention of the Austin press in early December that Jack Stick had resigned from his position of Chief Counsel at the Health and Human Services Commission.

They found out that he resigned because Kyle Janek had refused to spend a further $90 million on Medicaid fraud detection software from the Austin software firm, 21CT, that Stick had been championing. Stick had a year earlier convinced HHSC and the federal government to invest in the software for Texas OIG at a cost of $20 million.

Three problems with that. One, the company had no experience with Medicaid fraud detection and it was the first time its software had been deployed for that purpose. Two, the state's contract bidding process had been avoided by using a state program to approve contracts worth on average less than $4,000. Three, and what really brought down the house, Stick was found to have a relationship with 21CT CEO Irene Williams and a former business partner of Stick's, then a 21CT lobbyist, alleged that Stick was building up the company so he could leave state employ and take an executive position with the firm.

The fact that 21CT avoided the state bidding process brought catcalls from competitors and enraged everyone from the governor on down. The state auditor started an investigation. Governor Greg Abbott appointed a strike force to look into the situation and HHSC. The FBI showed interest.

The revelations about 21CT brought on further press scrutiny of what was going on in HHSC and more things were found. Commissioner Janek had given almost $100,000 to an aide so he could get his MBA in violation of state rules. There were calls for his resignation.

Doug Wilson was getting the 21CT software used in another department of HHSC, the one in which his wife was the director. This was the last straw for Doug Wilson.

Governor Perry, before he left office, asked Wilson for his resignation and got it.

When the dust settled, Stick, Wilson, and four more individuals had resigned. Commissioner Janek would last until May 2015 after all the investigations were done. He then handed in his resignation.

December 2014 was a black month for HHSC and its OIG.

But it was a great month for Medicaid providers!

Because Wilson and Stick were gone, the state dropped its appeal of the decision on returning my monies. Before Christmas, I received back some $1.2 million.

The state also took several Medicaid dental cases, including mine, and sent them to district court rather than floundering with OIG. I would get a jury trial.

It looked like justice was going to be served after all.

CHAPTER 14

THE SAGA CONTINUES

2015 was an exceptional year for changes for the better at the Texas Health and Human Services Commission and the Office of Inspector General.

After its hearings in December, the Sunset Advisory Commission went on to draft legislation to reform OIG, which was passed unanimously by the Texas Legislature and signed into law by Governor Abbott. Senate Bill 207 does the following:

- Provides timeframes for OIG to complete preliminary and full investigations.
- Requires OIG to conduct quality assurance reviews for its sampling methodology used in the investigative process.
- Limits OIG's ability to place payment holds in cases not involving fraud.
- Clarifies that "fraud" does not include unintentional technical, clerical, or administrative errors.

It also ended the odious practices of HHSC being able to change the rulings of administrative courts such as in the case of Dr. Nazari and Antoine Dental Centers and requiring Medicaid providers to pay court costs in advance to get a hearing.

This was a great victory for all Medicaid providers!

As another part of that reform, at the beginning of March, Governor Abbott appointed Stuart Bowen Jr. as the new inspector general for OIG. Bowen was the former special inspector general for Iraq Reconstruction and a former aide to George W. Bush, both when he was governor and president. He immediately started bringing order to the mess that was the Office of Inspector General and told the media and Medicaid providers that he wanted to work with providers to fix the system.

Throughout the year, he made quite a few changes. The largest was that he started settling outstanding investigations and cases late in the year.

This was a wise thing to do because in May, another dentist, Dr. Cheryl Rhoden, went before the State Office of Administrative Hearings on allegations of Medicaid fraud. The state lost again, big time. The administrative court judge not only dismissed the allegations of fraud against Dr. Rhoden, finding no evidence, but also awarded court costs to her. This is a very rare circumstance but it was warranted because the case should never have gotten so far.

Unfortunately for me and a few others, because our cases had been moved over to district court, these settlements were not available to us.

The biggest vindication yet, that the dentists were not the ones responsible for the large scale of spending on Medicaid orthodontic treatment between 2007 and 2012, came from a further federal audit of that spending released in May.

The audit division of the Department of Health and Human Services Office of Inspector General, following up on their previous audit, determined that the state of Texas owed back to the federal government some $133 million that had been paid for improperly approved Medicaid orthodontic treatment.

The agency even did a podcast about their report and put the blame for the fiasco firmly at the feet of the state. The auditor said the following as to why the situation occurred:

"Two reasons. First, the state agency did not ensure that the contractor properly reviewed each prior-authorization to make sure it was both medically necessary and that the beneficiary qualified for orthodontic services. Second, the state agency did not ensure the contractor's dental director followed state Medicaid policies and procedures for determining medical necessity and if a beneficiary qualified for orthodontic services."

Nothing about fraud committed by dentists!

The press had also changed.

In January, Texas Public Radio did an interview about the 21CT scandal with two key reporters from the *Texas Tribune* and the *Houston Chronicle*, Terri Langford and Brian Rosenthal. Because 21CT was focused on providing Medicaid fraud detection software, the topic of dental Medicaid fraud came up, particularly the orthodontic spending debacle. In contrast to what might have been said back in 2011, in answer to the host's question, Rosenthal said there was obviously some fraud in dental billings, "although there was a lot of questions about how much fraud was actually taking place." Langford concurred, saying, "Exactly."

We were in a new time and it was very gratifying.

But, you know, we are down the road another year as I am writing this book and I have to tell you I am still not out of the woods.

Nope.

In the last chapter I related that in December of 2015 my case and those of several others were transferred to district court after the departure of Jack Stick. This was to give us "justice" by going before a jury.

Well, it hasn't ended up that way so far. I am still waiting.

You might be thinking to yourself "So why is he writing this book now? The mess isn't over."

Totally true, but there are compelling reasons to get this book out.

It is basically a warning to other healthcare providers around the country about what can happen to them.

It is also a warning to citizens who care about such things that our government agencies can get out of control and that they will willy-nilly violate our constitutional rights in their seemingly mindless pursuit of their agendas.

But there is even a better reason.

The full truth of the matter is that the whole attack on dentists for the Medicaid orthodontic spending in Texas is, and has been from day one, politically motivated.

No one expected us to fight back. We were just supposed to pay up or go bankrupt with no one being the wiser.

I think that was Jack Stick and Doug Wilson's job—don't let the state government get blamed for the orthodontic spending mess.

It didn't work out because we did fight back! And we had the truth on our side!

So it is very important and timely to tell this story.

Now we get to the most important chapter of the book: what to do if it happens to you!

CHAPTER 15
SIX RULES TO FOLLOW

Yes, yes, it couldn't possibly happen to you or someone you love or someone you know.

But let's be prepared like we learned in scouting.

We had weathered the storm!

I believed in the power to make things go right by applying the ethical principles instilled in me by my parents and education. We did many things right and I want to share with you the lessons I learned along the way. All of them are simple and effective, so here they are:

1. BELIEVE IN YOURSELF

If you haven't done anything wrong, don't allow others to convince you otherwise. And don't start to believe the bad stuff yourself.

There was a tremendous amount of pressure in the early days to succumb to the idea that our practice must have done something wrong. Look at all the media exposés, look at the government investigations, look at what was happening to colleagues. The overwhelming public opinion was that dentists, including myself, were money-hungry fraudsters hurting fellow Texans. That is a tough pill to swallow when you have dedicated your entire life to helping others.

And it is something you can't be prepared for. I never thought in a million years that I would ever have to face such a situation. So when it did hit, I was almost swept off my feet because I couldn't believe it.

Your own personal integrity is the key to having a happy and successful life. You can also stand tall regardless of the severity of any situation you may face in life.

I must say that my military training helped too. God knows I have faced enormous obstacles in my life from early childhood to present time. Standing up to the government with its unlimited resources has been my biggest challenge. Having been trained to fight in the military, it was my biggest shock to find myself fighting my own government. I am glad to have had that training.

2. DON'T GO INTO HIDING; SPEAK UP!

Some guys, when they found they were under an unfair investigation, believed it was better to be quiet and "not rock the boat." They sort of felt ashamed even if they hadn't done anything wrong and worried what colleagues and others might think. Worse, they were worried about incurring further wrath from the authorities who were already trying to wipe out their practices.

Doesn't this already say something about the level of trust we have in our governments—that we expect revenge and sadistic treatment for "rocking the boat?" Anyway, I don't know what more wrath you could incur than what they were already leveling at us. These people, unfortunately, sort of disappeared and hid, hoping it would all blow over.

This wasn't tenable for me. If everyone was afraid, how would this situation get resolved? I found the only way was to be forthright about what was happening. I resolved to speak my mind openly and say what I thought was wrong and do something about it. I didn't do it in a way that was brash or disrespectful or created a scene. I did it in the way I felt was the most rational possible. It ended up working out.

3. SURROUND YOURSELF WITH GOOD PEOPLE

I was fortunate to find some great people who could help me deal with this situation. This was no accident; I looked and I listened. I know good advice when I hear it. It took a little believing at the beginning that it could be turned around but it worked out that way.

My legal team did an excellent job—attorneys Jason Ray, Oscar Garcia, Tony Canales, and Ricardo Barrera.

It also took a team of individuals on the public side to tell the story and get it to legislators and the media. These guys, George Mentis and Al Anthony of Target Public Marketing and Chuck Young, were primary.

I am also indebted to my colleagues in the Rio Grande Valley District Dental Society for their support, especially Dr. Jose Cazares, a past president and a fellow Medicaid dentist.

He steadfastly stood beside me as I went through my trials and tribulations. He is now in line to become the next president of the Texas Dental Association. The fact that the Rio Grande Valley District Dental Society passed a resolution to support our group, Texas Dentists for Medicaid Reform, cannot be forgotten. Their support is greatly appreciated.

Needless to say, part of this is forming a group that then promotes the truth to the public, your profession, the media, and the government. There is strength in numbers, even if the numbers aren't that great. Even a few good people make a great difference.

4. FIGHT BACK

There is a financial cost to fighting back. Pay it. It is money well spent if only for your own peace of mind. There is something that happens when you compromise your belief in yourself, even though there is vast pressure to do so.

Here are two examples:

A dentist in West Texas was criminally charged with Medicaid fraud. He pleaded guilty and went to prison. Once in prison, he started complaining about the fact that prosecutors had told him that if he didn't plead guilty, they were going to also charge his wife who worked in the practice and was his office manager. He had succumbed to the pressure and then regretted it later after it was way too late.

Another dentist whose story I am acquainted with was accused of a small dollar amount of Medicaid fraud. The state was seeking to get back less than $30,000. He said he was innocent but rather than fight, which he felt might be costly and bankrupt him and would only be a "hollow moral victory," as he put it, he paid back the money and pleaded no contest to a lowly, unspecified count of criminal mischief.

No fine, no incarceration, no sweat, no pain. It was all over ... except for the fact that by pleading no contest he destroyed his practice as he no longer qualified to be a Medicaid provider. He was barred from all federal healthcare programs.

Then he found out the state had closed the case against him, marking the file "not sufficient evidence." So he would have won if he had fought. But instead, he has been fruitlessly fighting for years to recover from this.

5. GO TALK TO LEGISLATORS

So you think all politicians are no good. That they won't listen. That they can't do anything anyway.

Well, you'll be in for a surprise. You'll find out you elected some pretty good and caring people. That's what I found out.

They did listen when I presented the facts and documentation and they did do something. They ended up reforming an agency out of control and forcing its rogue bureaucrats to resign.

It is gratifying to see what can happen when there is a cause everyone can get behind. Things do happen. Laws can be changed with enough public outcry for justice.

As a result, we have a better State of Texas today than we had four years ago. That's better for everyone.

6. PERSEVERE

This is the last and the hardest one to achieve. There are so many platitudes I could throw at you about this. But words are cheap when you are faced with a major, potentially career-ending situation and crippling financial burdens.

It sometimes takes months or even years for a light to become visible.

I've already related the story of Dr. Leonard Morris from New York who lost his practice and his home before, finally, many years later, getting a $7 million jury award against his accusers.

I am sure Dr. Morris felt his perseverance was worth it. It is pretty much a point of reputation, self-worth, and self-respect.

CHAPTER 16
LAST WORDS

The six points mentioned in the last chapter are simple to elucidate but harder to achieve. We each have our own journeys and hopefully you will never be in a position to have to apply them to a life situation of your own.

But America is only America if we keep it that way. When rogue bureaucrats and agencies start setting their own crooked agendas, the only ones who can stop it are those who are affected. If I had never spoken up, I'd be bankrupt now and those rogue bureaucrats would still be sitting in their cushy chairs, ruling over us.

Yes, it is hard. I wrote in the beginning about our cherished constitutional rights.

Well, they are only ours if we keep and maintain them. Sometimes we have to fight for them. It is up to "we, the people" in the end to have the kind of country we want to live in.

Perhaps such battles define us. Perhaps such travails are necessary to preserve the freedom our founding fathers wanted us to have. Perhaps such fights do not diminish our country but, in actuality, make it great.

It is a sign of hope that a single citizen can win against a government and state so huge that it has the twelfth largest economy in the world.

I was given the liberty and freedom to express my views and fight for my God-given rights as an American citizen. I will treasure and defend those rights for as long as I live.

God bless our great nation!

To contact Dr. Villarreal personally or for more information, please email Texas Dentists for Medicaid Reform at info@tdmr.org.

Harlingen Family Dentistry Staff

Harlingen Family Dentistry clinic with the children's clinic and specialty clinic comprising 26,000 sq ft and 63 dental chairs.

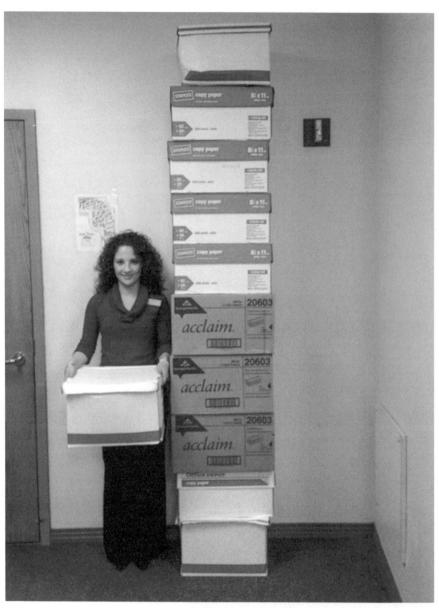

Marisol Alanis, Office Manager with records requested for general and pediatric patients after the State Office of Administrative Court Hearings found no fraud, waste, or abuse.

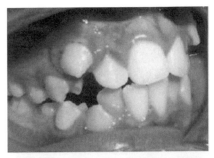
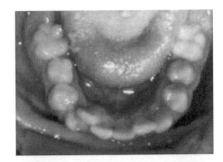
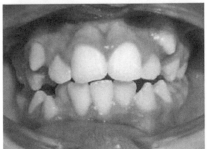
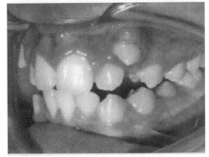

A picture of a child's teeth the expert
witness for OIG used to determine
that the patient did not need braces
and were not "medically necessary."

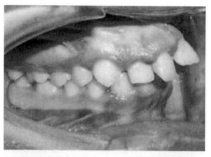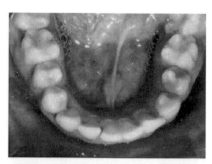
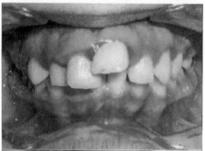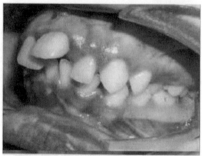

Pictures of another child's teeth the
OIG expert witness used to conclude
that the patient did not qualify as
"medically necessary" for braces.

Former Deputy Inspector General Jack Stick spent $5,600 on chairs for himself and his boss

THE TEXAS ACADEMY OF GENERAL DENTISTRY
is proud to acknowledge the nomination of

Juan D. Villarreal, DDS

for
Dentist of the Year
By the Rio Grande Valley Dental Society
2015

The Rio Grande Valley Dental
Society nominated me for the Texas
Academy of General Dentistry's
Dentist of the Year Award in 2015.

The State of Texas

to all to whom these presents shall come, Greetings: Know ye, that

Juan D. Villarreal

is hereby commissioned

Member,

State Board of Dental Examiners

(August 29, 2001)

under the laws of the State of Texas with all rights, privileges, and emoluments appertaining to said office. In testimony whereof, I have signed my name and caused the Seal of State to be affixed at the City of Austin on October 19, 2001.

Rick Perry
Governor of Texas

Geoffrey S. Connor
Assistant Secretary of State

My appointment to the State Board of Dental Examiners by Governor Rick Perry

Our annual Harlingen Family Dentistry JROTC Scholarship winners, participants and judges, including General Charles Rodriguez. Candidates demonstrate their commitment to community values through real world projects.